The Critical Idiom

General Editor: JOHN D. JUMP

27 Classicism

In the same series

Classicism/*Dominique Secretan*

Methuen & Co Ltd

First published 1973
by Methuen & Co Ltd
11 New Fetter Lane London EC4
© *1973 Dominique Secretan*
Printed in Great Britain
by Cox & Wyman Ltd, Fakenham, Norfolk

SBN 416 75010 9 Hardback
SBN 416 75020 6 Paperback

Distributed in the U.S.A. by

HARPER & ROW PUBLISHERS, INC.
BARNES & NOBLE IMPORT DIVISION

Contents

General Editor's Preface

This volume is one of a series of short studies, each dealing with a single key item, or a group of two or three key items, in our critical vocabulary. The purpose of the series differs from that served by the standard glossaries of literary terms. Many terms are adequately defined for the needs of students by the brief entries in these glossaries, and such terms will not be the subjects of studies in the present series. But there are other terms which cannot be made familiar by means of compact definitions. Students need to grow accustomed to them through simple and straightforward but reasonably full discussions of them. The purpose of this series is to provide such discussions.

Some of the terms in question refer to literary movements (e.g. 'Romanticism', 'Aestheticism', etc.), others to literary kinds (e.g. 'Comedy', 'Epic', etc.), and still others to stylistic features (e.g. 'Irony', 'The Conceit', etc.). Because of this diversity of subject-matter, no attempt has been made to impose a uniform pattern upon the studies. But all authors have tried to provide as full illustrative quotation as possible, to make reference whenever appropriate to more than one literature, and to compose their studies in such a way as to guide readers towards the short bibliographies in which they have made suggestions for further reading.

John D. Jump

University of Manchester

Preliminary Remark

There is no clear-cut definition of the term *classicism*. Encyclopaedias use phrases such as *an aesthetic tendency characterized by a sense of proportion, by a balanced and stable composition, by a search for formal harmony and by understatement; imitation of ancient writers; aversion to the exceptional; well-nigh exclusive interest in psychological and moral analysis; control of sensitivity and imagination; submission to rules governing specific kinds of writing*, and so on. *Classicism* has been equated with Beauty, with Reason, with Health, with Tradition. The term has been over-used by some, spurned by others.

Faced with the vast complex called *classicism*, I have not attempted to give a definition, large or small. I have merely looked into the numerous elements which enter into it: its backbone, its flesh, the spirit that quickens it. *Classicism* is one of the aesthetic streams that flow through the changing landscapes of history. I have picked out some landmarks, and staked out some of the limits. The subject-matter is inexhaustible and therefore over-defined: *classicism*, I found, I could tackle best in the short space allowed by throwing a little light on the multiplicity of its manifestations.

Classicism is not a set of outworn and readily catalogued values: it lives on in many modern works of art.

I
Introduction

In his *Book of the Courtier* (1528), Baldesar Castiglione shows how easy and natural it is for man to glorify the past, to say to himself that whatever his task, it could have been performed more readily in his grandfather's time! I, too, feel tempted to think that, even fifty years ago, a clear-cut and relatively simple definition of *classicism* could have been offered to the reader of the day. We have become more wary of definitions; we take fewer things for granted, on trust; we tend to look ever farther back in time for the beginnings of any given literary movement, to analyse its components more thoroughly, to examine all those aspects which make it less pure. Thus we talk, for instance, of the classicism of the Romantics and the romanticism of the Classics. The picture may be said to grow at the same time more precise and less clear. Our truth is more complex than our fathers' truth.

A further complication is added, artificially perhaps, by the decision to look at the *classical* periods of three countries, namely France, England and Germany (not to mention forerunners in Greece, Rome and Italy), to compare developments which were neither simultaneous, nor in any way identical, but which were nevertheless interrelated and which share a sufficient number of features for comparisons to be legitimate and worth while. This study is therefore meant to belong to the field of comparative literature.

Difficulty also arises in the choice to be made of material leading to some sort of definition of the terms *classical*, *classicism* and *neo-classicism*. Firstly, there is a vast amount of overlapping and repetition: it is therefore important to choose, in any given period and country, the most interesting and original utterances, such as are found in prefaces, essays, manifestos, and so on, as well as the most relevant pieces of creative writing (often plays) that either informed criticism or arose from it. Secondly, there is an equally vast amount of literature based on Greek and Roman themes, myths, plots, characters, and which can only be understood as modern *variations* (in the full sense of the term) on the live material of antiquity. For a writer to be inspired by Athens and Rome is not enough to be styled a *classic*, although most of the works we are about to scrutinize do explicitly or implicitly acknowledge these sources of inspiration.

Paradoxically, one could call nearly all Western European literature classical, for classical means first and foremost ordered and controlled, and all literature is an attempt at putting experience, large and small, in some sort of order, at rationalizing feelings, at systematizing random thought, at embellishing nature. Literature should help us understand nature, that is the world we live in, and ourselves. And yet, how much literature actually screens the reader from nature!

Traditional literary criticism teaches us to avoid over-large categories. *Divide et impera*, the Romans said and we comply by seeking a smaller field to which the term *classical* can be more meaningfully applied.

Classic, as we use it in everyday speech, means typical, exemplary (a classic case), of the highest class in its kind, and thus worthy of study and imitation, in school and otherwise; *classical* is chiefly used for the best writers of antiquity (as in classical scholarship); *classicism*: a way of writing or painting marked by serene beauty, taste, restraint, order and clarity. Sometimes the term *neo-classicism* is used to distinguish modern from Greek and Latin classicism. It might be preferable, as we shall see later, to reserve neo-classicism for the revival (or survival!) of classicism in the eighteenth century. Latin *classis* means class, group, subdivision; it is the rough equivalent of a word used by the scholars working in the famous library at Alexandria, namely *canones*, i.e. genres of writing, writers arranged in groups (orators, playwrights, lyric poets, etc.). French *classique* and *classicisme* are readily understood. When we say *les classiques français*, we normally mean the great writers who created their masterpieces in the second half of the seventeenth century, under the aegis of the Sun-King, Louis xiv. *Classicism*, we remember, has undertones: stale formalism, lack of spontaneity, coldness. The same can be said of the German *Klassizismus*. *Klassisch* presents no semantic problems; *die grossen Klassiker* denotes writers of the calibre of Goethe and Schiller. Whenever the terms just listed occur in literary history, we oppose them, mentally at least, to *romantic* and *Romanticism*, as well as to *baroque* (noun and adjective).

'He who seeks to define Romanticism is entering a hazardous occupation which has claimed many victims' (E. B. Burgum, quoted by Lilian Furst in *Romanticism*, 'The Critical Idiom'). The same could be said of Classicism; and yet, there is no need for despondency. We must have definitions, even if they are hard to come by, even if they are not final or entirely satisfactory, even if they remain merely working hypotheses . . .

Classical is for us a convenient pointer-word for a particular attitude to life. There are, I think, two ways of looking at the human condition. The first starts with a number of questions: what is life about? where is it taking us? how can we go beyond what we already know? to what extremes can life go? how can I express the fullness of a full life? The attitude characterized by these questions and others we might call forward-looking, experimental, imaginative, fearless; it is often formless, because it does not rest anywhere, and because it is always looking for new forms of expressing new visions. It contains much of what is to be found in many traditional definitions or descriptions of Romanticism.

The other basic attitude begins with another set of questions: what has the past taught us? what do we share with the generations that have gone before us, with the nations around us? how best can we sum up what was, is and perhaps will be? what is unchanging Nature really like? We have here a mode of thinking more rational, more synthetic, more static, which tends to systematize, to accept what is of proven value, to make use of forms handed down from generation to generation. And for the purpose of this study, we shall call this second attitude *classical*.

In each of us there are classical and romantic elements: a sane person and one diseased (to retain Goethe's terminology). To separate them in any individual may be a futile task, but as literature reflects these tendencies on a large scale, the distinction becomes meaningful: facets of our intimate life magnified and generalized, mirrors held up to the life of a nation. To distinguish, to grasp *otherness*, to become more tolerant. . . .

Both movements under scrutiny have a past. The student of Romanticism cannot help reflecting on the impact made by the Middle Ages and the Gothic on pre-romantic and romantic writers, and, for that matter on the main stream of English literature which is not classical in essence. The student of Classicism, on the other hand, must perforce cast his eyes back to antiquity, for it is there, in Greece and Rome, that the sixteenth, seventeenth and eighteenth centuries, to a greater or lesser degree, found their sources of inspiration. Classicism always looks back, when it theorizes and when it creates. It is to the classical *golden age* and its lessons that we now turn.

La Bruyère, in the late seventeenth century, opened his famous *Characters* with the pithy statement: *Tout est dit*. 'All is said (. . .) we can but glean after the ancients and the most skilful among the moderns', implying the most skilful imitators of the great classics. Imitation is one of the key-words we shall come across frequently, a word our century despises, but to which, if it is correctly interpreted, we owe some very beautiful pieces of creative writing! For La Bruyère, imitation is no slavish aping, for it is possible to imitate nothing but a spirit of truth, a high degree of excellence, a faithfulness to a stable and reasonable philosophy of life. For a classic, only the fundamentals of the mind (reason, the sundry faculties, basic feelings, certain vices and virtues) remain unchanging throughout the course of time, whereas life-styles, factors external to man, moral climates, the sensitivity of successive generations, knowledge of the universe, all evolve, together with their modes of expression: 'Horace and Despréaux (Boileau) said it before us; but I say it in my own way.' (La Bruyère)

Many of the books we are about to encounter are not, in the words of Chesterton, 'cold and monumental like a classical tomb', in which might lie but an unfeeling heart!

To illustrate another important point, let us consider the fate of Theophrastus, the disciple and successor of Aristotle at the school of philosophy in Athens. From among Theophrastus' voluminous works, only one, a slim collection of character sketches, has come down to us, but the story of the influence exerted by these *Characters* (written around 320 B.C.) is curious and relevant to our study.

There are, broadly speaking, two kinds of portrait a painter or writer can execute (omitting the further distinction between realistic, idealized and satirical portraits): the one portrays a particular and unique individual, the other describes a type. Artists in general (to introduce another very broad distinction) prefer the first kind, moralists the second, for the simple reason that the moralist (the psychologist) moves in a more overtly scientific way; he wants to pass on to his students, useful and generalized information concerning man. The same can be said of the preacher-moralist who castigates vice in general terms, by means of types: the Greedy man, the Boorish man, the Liar and so on. The characters of Theophrastus are all *deviants*, extremes, people who do not conform to the morality or the manners of their society, who do not conform to the Aristotelian *mean* of behaviour. They were meant to be studied in the class of rhetoric (rhetoric being the study of all the available means of influencing others). In other words they were to provide the orator with illustrative material, just as figures of speech, proverbs, etc., were studied for use at the appropriate moment. (*The Characters* is available in 'Penguin Classics'.)

Theophrastus had many imitators and commentators both in Greece and in Rome. His method was passed on to the Scholastics in the Middle Ages, and then on to the moralists of the Renaissance. Character-writing was then known as *Descriptio*. *Descriptio* was practised in England before the first famous Latin version and commentary appeared in 1592, published in Geneva by Casaubon, a kind of latter-day Theophrastus. This was translated into English by John Healey and published in 1616. Now it could be claimed that the subsequent craze (in England and in France) for the portrait, the character, the ἤθη, was due to the mediation of Casaubon, and Healey. This however is not strictly true, for, as we have just seen, the tradition of the *Descriptio* had never been lost. Furthermore, the first great exponent of the genre in England, Joseph Hall, had in 1608 already brought out his *Characters of Virtues and Vices*.

Thus, 'the *Character*, already familiar as a rhetorical form, was re-established in England as a definite gift of the ancient to the modern world, and when it entered on its hundred years of popularity, carried on it, definitely stamped, the name of Theophrastus' (G. S. Gordon, 'Theophrastus and his Imitators', in *English Literature and the Classics*, Oxford 1912.)

My aim in mentioning the *Characters* is obviously not to write the history of the genre (as exemplified by Sir Thomas Overbury,

John Earl, Cleveland, Butler, Addison and others (who did not necessarily all have first-hand knowledge of Theophrastus), and by La Bruyère (to whom we owe a French translation) and his predecessors and successors in France); nor to show the close links existing between the *Characters* and the obtaining moral theory (the Aristotelian 'mean', the 'theory of humours', the concept of 'l'honnête homme', of the 'man of sense'); nor to point out the conjunction with comedy (Theophrastus–Menander; Roman moralists – Plautus and Terence; Hall and others – Ben Jonson; La Bruyère – Molière; Addison – Congreve); nor the obvious links with the essay (Bacon, Montaigne). What should be stressed is that filiations from ancient to modern are never simple or straightforward, that they simultaneously follow different routes: via texts extant, texts lost and recovered, commentaries, oral tradition, cross-fertilization, grafting of indigenous products on to classical themes. The problems of influence and filiation are always arduous, especially as writers often acknowledge unimportant sources, omit important ones and remain unaware of others. (The Romantic Maurice de Guérin never even mentioned Senancour, to whom he owed so much!)

A further point, however obvious, has to be made at this stage. In the movement under scrutiny, the classicism of the moderns, theory will appear to play an inordinately big part. The literary works of the seventeenth and eighteenth centuries in France, of the Augustan age in England, of the eighteenth century in Germany, feed on the writings of theorists. Theory and practice go hand in hand, for better or worse, and many poets are also well known for their prefaces and critical essays (Dryden and Corneille, to mention but two). The reason for this marriage will become apparent as we proceed. It may be enough to say here, that what underlies classicism is partly a theory of imitation, partly an immoderate faith in Reason.

.   .   .   .   .

It is becoming apparent, as we circumscribe the notion of classicism, that its study is strewn with obstacles and can quite easily lead us up the proverbial garden path. The sequence of events may be misleading, with assumed filiations stated too categorically, others omitted, and works interpreted outside the moral climate which informs them or against which they stand.

Another difficulty can best be illustrated by the problems arising from what is called neo-platonism. According to J. A. Stewart ('Platonism in English Poetry', in *English Literature and the Classics*), Platonism is 'the mood of one who has a curious eye for the endless variety of this visible and temporal world and a fine sense of its beauty, yet is haunted by the presence of an invisible and eternal world behind, or ... within, the visible and temporal world, and sustaining both it and himself ... from love of the visible and temporal, he is lifted up to love of the invisible and eternal world.' This invisible world of ideas (Goodness, Truth and Beauty), this God, operates through a hierarchy of beings upon every particle of matter. Three of Plato's works in particular, *Phaedon*, *Symposium*, and *Timaeus*, embody this deeply-felt *idealism* of the philosopher, who exerted a powerful influence on poets, thinkers, religious men, 'Pagan, Jewish, Christian and Moslem, through the Alexandrine period and the early centuries of our era, through the dark ages – so called – through the two centuries of the dawning Renaissance, till in the latter half of the fifteenth century, with the foundation of the Platonic Academy at Florence, his personality became the object of a cult'. The dialogues 'translated and commented on by the chief devotee of this cult, Marsilio Ficino ... now began to be read in the West'. This influence is felt in Dante, Petrarch, the Renaissance poets, Spenser, Sidney, Shakespeare, Jonson, Donne and in Wordsworth and the Romantics (perhaps even in Alain Fournier's *Le Grand Meaulnes* ...). (It is appropriate at this point to refer the reader to Arthur O. Lovejoy's *The Great*

Chain of Being and also to the *Continental Renaissance*, quoted below.)

Here then is a movement, which has clearly a single source in antiquity, namely Plato's mystical experience of a conjoined duality, of a world seen and of a world inferred or recollected – a stream of works inspired by the Plato who was not laying down any laws or giving any precepts but who handed down a vision. Yet classicism as such, was not affected by this vision. It did not, broadly speaking, include in its waters the stream of Platonism (or neo-Platonism as we might call it since the advent of Ficino).

The lesson to be learned from this brief excursion is twofold. Firstly, classicism does not necessarily feed on all the theories or works of the ancients. And although lovers of literature cannot fail to find traces of Platonism or neo-Platonism in the writings to be discussed, they will have to bear with us when we come to focus our attention on Aristotle, Horace and Longinus, to the detriment of the more deeply moving Plato. Secondly we must remain aware of the fact that in matters of literature there are two vastly different kinds of sources of inspiration – the works of the *poets* (plays, stories, poems, speeches, meditations and so on) and the works of the critics (literary or moral critics, aesthetes, law-givers good and bad, commentators of different waters, etc.) In the case of Horace (as of many moderns) the two types are combined; in the case of Aristophanes the plays include a criticism of other play-wrights. The neo-classicists we are dealing with were influenced to some measurable degree, both by the creative and by the theoretical works of the past (or at least by the theories elaborated in the sixteenth and seventeenth centuries by Italian and French commentators of Aristotle). Anouilh cannot be considered a disciple of the classics merely because he treats afresh the old theme of *Antigone*; a number of other characteristics must also be present.

B

2
Italian Renaissance – Greece and Rome

By the time Marsilio Ficino (who had sought to reconcile Platonism and Christianity) died in 1499, most of the important literary works of antiquity had been made available to the Italian people and the rest of Europe, in Latin translation and with copious commentaries, thanks mainly to the labours of Valla, Pico della Mirandola, Vida, Poliziano and Ficino himself. Linguistic studies were well advanced and improved texts were put before a public for whom the Latin language held few mysteries. (The same benefits were imparted to Patristic writings. Erasmus is one of the chief exponents of the renewal of Bible studies.) The typical man of the Renaissance is the Humanist with his enthusiastic concern for science, travelling and the past in all its aspects; he stressed man's self-reliance, a self-reliance tempered by Platonism and propped up ethically by the stoicism taught in Epictetus' *Manual* (translated into Latin in 1498): a code of self-help and self-mastery, the influence of which was to be felt far into the more specifically classical age. For him, one feels, life is an art, such as is depicted, for example, in *The Book of the Courtier* by Castiglione. The Frenchman Jacques Amyot's and the Englishman North's translations of Plutarch's *Lives* (1559) did a great deal to foster that interest in an already remote past; just as Cicero's and Seneca's works added much fuel to the discussion of stylistic and moral questions.

It would be tempting to retrace, however rapidly, the story of the Renaissance, but we must limit ourselves to certain more relevant aspects of Renaissance criticism, which alone can allow for the classicism of the seventeenth century, and refer interested readers to *The Continental Renaissance* (edited by A. J. Krailsheimer) from which I take a single sentence: 'By 1600 the movement which had begun in Italy some 150 years before had led to the establishment everywhere of a recognized educational system based on a sound command of Latin and Greek, bringing down to our own day the common cultural heritage of ancient history, mythology and wisdom.'

The Renaissance stands not only for a renewal of classical scholarship, but also for successful attempts at elevating the vernacular to a proper vehicle for literature. In Italy, grammar books were written and dictionaries compiled, language standardized, under the aegis of Academies (long before Richelieu founded the ponderous Académie Française in 1635). The French followed suit, and Du Bellay gave his famous *Défense et Illustration de la Langue Française* (1549). So the 'Questione della Lingua' exercised the Italian mind most successfully, yet what exercised it equally were certain texts of Aristotle, his *Rhetoric* and his *Poetics* (whereas the Middle Ages had given their attention mainly to Aristotle's logic and philosophy). It therefore seems appropriate to recall some of the utterances, precepts, comments or whatever we want to call them, of some of the fathers of literary criticism, Aristotle, Horace and Longinus, without the knowledge of which the tenets of neo-classicism remain incomprehensible.

Aristotle had of course had predecessors, whose 'rudimentary form of literary criticism' (to use T. S. Dorsch's formula in *Classical Literary Criticism*, Penguin Books, which includes Aristotle's *Poetics*, Horace's *Art of Poetry* and Longinus' *On the Sublime*) can be studied in J. W. H. Atkins' *Literary Criticism in Antiquity*. The most interesting utterances among these are those embodied in Aristophanes' own comedies (in particular, in *The Frogs*, where the respective merits of Aeschylus and Euripides are carefully weighed up). From the Plato-Socrates arguments, we can only afford to consider here those which go to show that art and poetry are an illusion, an imitation: *mimesis*, which Plato at first condemned but later accepted, provided that the epic and dramatic poets concentrated on worthy subjects. Plato's attitude to Art remained ambiguous, although his vast scheme of things was charged with poetry. (Many of his works containing literary criticism are available as 'Penguin Classics'.)

Aristotle is not always explicit and, more important, is never as categorical as has been claimed by some who were perhaps over-impressed by his methodical approach. In the *Poetics* he gives advice to the budding playwright, and, at the same time, gives him plenty of scope and latitude. He expects the poet to be more than a historian or a slavish imitator: he wants him to reach for some universal truth, to build up a convincing plot about the downfall of a worthy man, a complex plot with a twist, such as a sudden reversal or a discovery. The action should be motivated by thought and character. Here are four quotations which typify the approach:

> Tragedy then is a representation of an action that is worth serious attention, complete in itself and of some amplitude, in language enriched by a variety of artistic devices appropriate to the several parts of the play; presented in the form of action, not narration; by means of pity and fear, bringing about the expurgation of such emotion. By language that is enriched, I refer to language possessing rhythm, and music or song; and by artistic devices appropriate to the several parts I mean that some are produced by the medium of verse alone and others again with the help of song.
>
> If the poet has depicted something impossible, he is at fault indeed, but he is justified in doing it as long as the art attains its true end, as I have described it, that is, as long as it makes this, or some part of the poem, more striking.
>
> Tragedy tries as far as possible to keep within a single revolution of the sun, or only slightly to exceed it, whereas the epic observes no limits in its time of action.
>
> Whatever is beautiful, whether it be a living creature or an object

made up of various parts, must necessarily, not only have its parts properly ordered, but also of an appropriate size, for beauty is bound up with size and order.

Aristotle has nothing to say concerning the unity of place (though the chorus in Greek tragedy seems to make vast shifts in space undesirable; see *The Death of Tragedy* by George Steiner).

So much then for the aims of tragic poetry and the means employed to attain them. A law of the genre: a tragedy must end badly; a moral purpose: a warning is given to the spectator (it could happen to you!); an ideal: a play must be beautiful and convincing; a piece of advice: keep to certain limits, within the bounds of reason; a preference: tragedy is superior to epic poetry and history. *Expurgation of emotion, catharsis,* has never been convincingly explained: it might induce release of pent-up energy in the spectator, thus allowing for a more reasonable approach to crisis in real life. Aristotle's emphasis on plot over character (character reveals itself through the action) has an existential ring about it and the whole of the *Poetics* impresses one as being very much alive, that is, experimental.

Horace, in his *Art of Poetry*, is more chatty, less formal. He admires the Greeks, and wants poets to learn their craft from them. An admirer, yes, but no slavish imitator. For him poetry is an art that can be learned; a craft that should exert a civilizing influence. What he stresses particularly is the notion of *decorum*, propriety of thought and subject-matter, a fusion of all the parts of the poem, a fairly strict adherence to usage, notably in matters of language.

Admiration of the ancients, decorum and consistency within the work of art and craftmanship, these are the hall-marks of this verse epistle. From his *Epistle to Augustus*, we gather that Horace did not think it impossible for new poets to rival the ancients, a point many neo-classicists did not easily acknowledge!

The following quotations sum up some of his teaching:

It is usage which regulates the laws and conventions of speech.

You must give your days and nights to the study of Greek models.

Either follow the beaten track, or invent something that is consistent with itself.

And, more memorably:

Poets aim at giving either profit or delight, or at combining the giving of pleasure with some useful precepts for life.

On the Sublime is at one and the same time the title of, and the key to the work of Longinus (if he was, indeed, the author of the book). This *sublimity* implies greatness of aim and of means of execution, grandeur, purity, anything which contributes to making a writer famous; excellence aimed at delighting the reader. It is akin to enthusiasm and genius. 'Sublimity is the echo of a noble mind', it is 'the emulation and imitation of the great historians and poets of the past'. The sources of what is conducive to Sublimity are laid down in detail. Thanks to its practical illustrations, *On the Sublime* is one of the first primers in literary criticism which shows the 'superiority of flawed sublimity to flawless mediocrity'. Two more quotations from the text will suffice for our purpose:

Art is perfect only when it looks like nature, and again nature hits the mark only when she conceals the art that is within her.

Now the homely term is sometimes more expressive than elegant diction, for being taken from everyday life, it is at once recognized, and carries more conviction from its familiarity.

This list of salient points, taken from three thinkers whom the Italian Renaissance theorists (and after them the French, English and German neo-classicists) were to exploit to a degree that baffles us, does not take into account the studies of rhetoric undertaken by Aristotle, Cicero, Quintilian and others. Even a cursory glance at this rather specialized subject would take us too far.

If the spirit of the Renaissance still excites us, it is undoubtedly for its inquisitiveness and the enthusiasm with which it fastened on to every manifestation of life which faced it. Italian scholars of the sixteenth century however, did not merely admire, but having agreed upon the validity of literature conceived in the vernacular (with Dante, Petrarch and Boccaccio as the models worthy of imitation) they also groped towards a formulation of literary rules which would be as binding for Italian writers as were the so-called rules derived from Cicero, etc., for those writing in Latin. Each theorist would of course base his work mainly on one Greek or Roman critic. I would not be justified in giving here more than the briefest summary of Renaissance criticism. I refer the reader to:

a. René Bray, *La Formation de la Doctrine Classique en France;*
b. G. Saintsbury, *History of English Criticism* (London, 1911);
c. J. W. H. Atkins, *Literary Criticism in Antiquity* (followed by *The Medieval Phase, The Renascence,* and *Seventeenth and Eighteenth Centuries*), and
d. The Continental Renaissance, quoted above.

Any history of what has been called the *break with medievalism* should begin with Pico della Mirandola (*On the Dignity of Man,* 1496), Ficino and Valla (*On Pleasure,* 1431), for they all testify to a new spirit of enquiry, to the emancipation of reason and a search for a synthesis of all knowledge. If and when they attack (classical) authority, it is only because, in their scale of values, nature and/or reason prevail over accepted views, however sacred these views may be. Furthermore, it is blatantly true that these thinkers and linguists were typical of their age in so far as they wished all their efforts to be seen to contribute to a liberal education based on the study of languages and literature. Usefulness, as Atkins shows so well, was a criterion brought to bear on literary criticism, as on most other objects of enquiry. There were many therefore who elaborated rules, which could be imparted to the novice. For literature means wisdom, wisdom means good conduct, wisdom fosters prudence, just as rules lead (might lead?) to good literature. Reason, life and creative writing come full circle.

(Readers interested in the links between education, oratory and stylistics, grammar and rhetoric, plugged *ad nauseam* by the Renaissance as being the golden door to literature and its interpretation, will turn to W. H. Woodward's *Vittorio da Feltro and other Humanist Educators* (Cambridge, 1887) and Peter Dixon's *Rhetoric* (Methuen, 1971).)

There is no single literary doctrine which emerges clearly from the works either of the poets (as all writers were called at one time) or of the theorists. For Poliziano (cf. *Opera*, 1537–39), Cicero is not, as he is for others, the only perfect model. Neither for him nor for Bruni is poetry in any way dangerous to morals, as it was held to be by some. The disagreement whether Homer or Virgil was the greater, and on the nature of poetry, manifests itself in the theories pertaining to the dramatic poem. One common belief stands out and is summed up by René Bray in this way: 'All the works of the Italian theorists are based on the assumption that there are rules the poet must know and perforce use if he wants to succeed.'

The most important theorists were Minturno, Castelvetro and Scaliger. Vida's influence lasted until Boileau, but his ideas on epic poetry and the superiority of Virgil, though interesting, do not concern us here. In 1559, in *De Poeta*, Minturno sums up more or less what was to be the classical doctrine as understood by the seventeenth century: poetry must instruct and please, art (=hard work) is as necessary as genius or inspiration; the ancients are models worthy of imitation; tragedy must induce admiration; the different genres are subject to known rules.

Castelvetro is important here, mainly for having presented a clear picture of the unities (time, place, action) and for having systematized the theory of verisimilitude (*vraisemblance*). Scaliger, the most influential of the group, perhaps also the most level-headed, was a great partisan of the imitation of Virgil and of nature and a believer in common sense (reason) and hard work as leading more or less infallibly to literary success.

The Unities

a. Whereas the first half of the sixteenth century accepted that the time of the action should not exceed one day, the second half tended to reduce it to twelve hours (such points did matter at the time and went on mattering!). Scaliger pushed the theory to its logical conclusion: time of performance = more or less time of action in real life. Castelvetro agrees in theory (as the play is subject to control by the senses and verisimilitude must be preserved); in practice he allows for an action covering a time span of twelve hours.

b. Castelvetro, not apparently expecting great changes in scenery, postulates a single place for the action: 'Tragedy must have as subject-matter an action that happens in a reduced space and a short span of time, namely in the place and time *when the actors are performing.*'

c. Unity of action was probably the only unity that mattered to Aristotle: 'The fable must imitate a single complete action, the parts of which are disposed in such a fashion that not one of them can be shifted or removed without upsetting and spoiling the whole.' Most Italian critics were agreed on that. Castelvetro (and this was original) based the demand for unity of action on those for unity of time and space; he actually allowed two linked actions in one play.

d. Horace had inherited from Aristotle the following moral imperatives. The *mores* of the characters have to be fitting to the situation (of the characters), resembling (i.e. in agreement with what history teaches us about the characters), and

consistent (within the play). Aristotle had strongly emphasized the need for moral excellence, applied to all the characters or to the hero only. Castelvetro plumped for the second
alternative (so that the hero would excite sufficient pity in the
audience).

e. All this is linked up to, and in keeping with, Horace's demand
for decorum at all times. With his usual common sense, he
claimed that 'concerning poetry, what seems likely (though it
be impossible) is preferable to the unlikely (though it be true)'.
Absolute, historical truth is not required, only verisimilitude
(the criterion of which remains, after all, opinion, or consensus
of opinion). We have the impression that for him, psychological versimilitude matters much more than what is materially
possible.

f. For Aristotle, a tragedy must be stirring, it must contain what
the French called 'le merveilleux', something to marvel at. Nor
did subsequent critics quibble with this. Castelvetro agreed too
with the proviso that what is not credible cannot stir up that
awe that a good play should induce. We might profit by looking
at all this from a different angle. For Scaliger, tragedy is the
representation of an illustrious event ending in death, involving
high born characters and including a moral lesson clearly spelt
out (stoical or Christian); the models proposed are Seneca's
tragedies; decorum is to be preserved, according to the standards laid down by Horace or Virgil (Homer being considered
too crude). Art imitates and improves on Nature.

Castelvetro, on the other hand, stresses delight rather than
moral aims. His *rules* bear out the exigencies of the stage and
of the performance. Realistically, as always, he looks upon
Aristotle's scattered utterances, as nothing more than a
reasonable starting-point, thus allowing the playwright a
certain latitude.

(Guarini's tragi-comedy *Pastor Fido* 1590, is the typical

example of a forward-looking aesthetic attitude and should be compared with Giraldi's Senecan tragedy, *Canase*, 1542.)

Such were the ideas which so much taxed the minds of the Italians in the sixteenth century, and which were similarly to tax those of the French theorists of the seventeenth.

More quotations, more points made by many other critics, would only confuse the issue. The elaboration of the classical doctrine is made up of an endless chain, a mutation and permutation of a small number of terms.

The direct beneficiary and propagator in Europe of the Italian theorists was Daniel Heinsius, whose treatise *De tragoediae constitutione* (1611) ('the quintessence of Aristotle's *Art of Poetry*') became an important textbook for seventeenth-century classicism.

3
England before the Restoration

In the sixteenth century, literary critics in France and England, had a number of preoccupations which we need not go into here. Evaluation of the Greek and Roman texts that were becoming available at the time, did, of course, foster discussion; and Greece did not fail to influence playwrights. Neo-platonism was in full swing. The concerns of Humanism were the same all over Western Europe, but the urgent topics of the day had little to do with Italian theories of the theatre and with epic poetry; they encompassed problems of language (growth and classification), rhetoric, the art of persuasion and the nature of poetry.

Little need be said on specific critics, other than Philip Sidney and Ben Jonson.

Sir Philip Sidney's *Apology for Poetry* (1595), impassioned and to our taste a little cloying, and too moralistic, draws examples from all realms of knowledge. Providing that poetry is morally uplifting, Sidney sees no harm in the poets' embellishing nature and surpassing it. Scaliger is mentioned, as well as Minturno, whose terms 'admiration and commiseration' he prefers to the Aristotelian 'pity and fear'. He praises *Gorboduc* by Sackville and Norton as climbing to the height of Seneca's style, but criticizes its structure, 'for it is faulty both in place and time, the two necessary companions of all corporal action'. It is typical of Sidney's broad-mindedness that in his opinion, art is not subservient to history: 'and do they not know that a tragedy is tied to the laws of poesy, and not of history'. Furthermore, there is no need to explain to the audience all that has occurred before the main action, the crisis, begins. Comedy is admirably analysed (see p. 47

in *English Critical Essays*, edited by E. D. Jones). Sidney postulates a more refined kind of comedy which would delight and not merely raise a laugh. (How near we are already to Molière's conception of comedy as exemplified by the *Misanthrope*. Lyly had already asked for comedy to move *inward delight*.) He would like the subject matter to revolve around characters afflicted by certain human failings; the following century took up that suggestion with excellent results. Basically, Sidney has no objection to the relatively new tragi-comedy, or, furthermore, to a reasonable mixture of genres (this last point would tend to exclude him from the purer classicists). Loftiness, concentration, art that is something more than imitation, comedy of humours, these are truly classical features.

When Castelvetro's *Poetics* became known in England, it was too late, considering the successes of Marlowe, Kyd and of course Shakespeare, to give the English theatre a more classical bent. Classicism was never, it must be admitted, one of the main pre-occupations of English playwrights and audiences, despite the keen classicism of Ben Jonson. (I am not trying to minimize the influence of the ancient writers, only that of the Italian and English theorists, such as Grimaldi in the preface to his tragi-comedy *Christus Redivivus* in the middle of the sixteenth century or Ascham in his *Schoolmaster*.)

Elizabethan art, at least that which has survived, is experimental, very free, in the spirit of Lope de Vega (1562–1635), powerful, varied, unafraid of mixing the sublime with the ridiculous, often sensational, *romantic* as some call it, or baroque. Basically, it owes little to the Continent, and it appeals to popular taste. Above all, it aims at authenticity. A Shakespeare play is its own criterion, it cannot truly be measured in terms of a theory, and Shakespeare gave none. The tragic or comic material finds its own form: which, as was remarked earlier on, is the only classic feature to be found, if one dare embark on a generalization of such magnitude. (For hints on literary criticism in Shakespeare's plays, see Atkins, op. cit., ch.8.). The question whether tragedy teaches a moral is left to the spectator, who is merely offered a 'mirror held up to nature'.

After the many poets and scholars whose works contain at least part of the classical doctrine, after Sidney in particular, we encounter Ben Jonson. *Timber* or *Discoveries Made Upon Man and Matter, as they Flowed out of his Daily Reading* (1620–1635, published posthumously in 1640–1641), embodies the spirit, and more facets of the doctrine than any previous writing in England. This is partly because Jonson knew the *De Tragoediae constitutione* by Heinsius. Jonson became, so to speak, the new mouthpiece of Aristotle; yet he remained, to use Atkins' phrase, a liberal classicist. He tried to present a synthesis of, or a compromise between, England's native genius, and the best that antiquity had bestowed. Except for the 'sordid and vile', nothing is unworthy of consideration, although he is not always above some crudity himself. The epithet that suits him best is probably *pure*: implying good taste, 'pure and neat language', polished, lucid, well-ordered and well-proportioned prose or verse. His demand for clarity and intelligibility makes him prefer the brevity of wit to the complexity of Donne's conceits. I see him as the product of the 'town', with ironical undertones, with a special taste for the epigram, an intellectual genre for a sophisticated society. (He himself called his collected *Epigrams* the ripest of his studies.) His lyrics and masques are part and parcel of courtly entertainment. Restraint and control may be features of his mental make-up, but there is no doubt that familiarity with the ancients contributed to the urbanizing of his century.

Classical precepts remained for him a starting point, they taught judgement, the art of leaving nothing to chance, of moving freely between the bombastic and the colourless; for him, imitation stood for re-creation; the permanent principle of art is harmony. Precept and practice go hand in hand; 'No precept will profit a fool.' 'I must bring my precepts into practice.'

Earlier on, Jonson had stressed moral education, listed the subjects to be treated and extolled the idea of justice in tragedy (rather than the inducing of pity and fear). But he preferred to write comedy and to deal with follies (each character endowed with his own, according to his humour, choleric, sanguine, melancholic or phlegmatic) rather than with crime and punishment. In practice, Jonson sometimes broke the classical rules, and he felt it incumbent upon himself to apologize for these failings.

The young Jonson had felt the pull of the *classic*; older, he had accepted the challenge and reached what was for him a satisfactory compromise solution.

Ben Jonson strikes us as a level-headed, self-disciplined intellectual whose work reveals little of the man, as an artist for whom reason and order are the tools needed for pleasing, for imposing a simple moral truth (that suffered at the hand of falsehood, shallow opinion, imagination, vices, follies, etc), and as fighting rebellion against a balanced view of life. Also as a theorist who believed, however, 'that any theory should be tested against experience' (J. B. Bamborough's phrase, in *Ben Jonson*, Hutchinson, 1970). Versatile, he drew as much from his native heritage as from Terence, Plautus, Aristophanes, Horace and Juvenal and from the exponents of classical doctrine. His particular blend of control and exuberance, of strict framework and ornamentation, make any clear distinction between baroque (or Englishness?) and classicism particularly difficult.

He has been likened to Molière, and it is true that his comedies have had a more lasting influence than his tragedies: devoid of a tragic view of life, Jonson did not lack the rare quality of ironic perspective.

The spirit of this early English classicism is well formulated by Atkins:

Of the ancient principles thus revived, the most notable was perhaps the fundamental and indispensable need for clear thinking, as opposed to concentration on formal artifice or tortured phrase. And this was accompanied by further demands for an orderly development of thought with easy transitions, for a diction and a manner in keeping with the theme, the occasion and the reader, as well as for a discreet use of those figurative devices in which human emotion has always found artistic expression. Apart from this, the necessity for constant practice and a concealment of art, was also inculcated; style, it was pointed out, was inevitably an expression of personality, and its highest qualities were said to be realized, not in an array of flowers, but in order, proportion, simplicity, and above all, perspicuity. As Quintilian long ago had stated, the aim in writing should be 'not merely to enable the reader to understand, but to make it impossible for him not to understand'.

(*Renascence*, p. 347)

The schools we attend in our youth leave on us an indelible mark, for better or worse, and this love–hate relationship goes a long way, in some cases at least, towards explaining certain basic trends in many great thinkers. Milton's school was St Paul's where he was influenced by the humanist curriculum devised by Colet and Erasmus, and where he learnt to strive for the best. Through the Spanish humanist Vives, perhaps, Erasmus had known of Longinus and *The Sublime*. Longinus, Vives, Erasmus and now Milton, each in his own way stands for greatness, breadth of vision, perfection. Their interests lie in 'what was always, everywhere, appreciated by all'; in one word, universality. Two quotations seem particularly relevant:

The measure is English heroic verse without rime, as that of Homer in Greek, and of Virgil in Latin – rime being no necessary adjunct or true ornament of poem or good verse, in longer works especially, but the invention of a barbarous age . . . This neglect then of rime . . . is to be esteemed an example set – the first in English – of ancient liberty recovered to heroic poem from the troublesome and modern bondage of riming.

(Preliminary note to *Paradise Lost.*)

They only will best judge who are not unacquainted with Aeschylus, Sophocles and Euripides, the three tragic poets unequalled yet by any, and the best rule to all who endeavour to write tragedy. The circumscription of time ... is, according to ancient rule and best example, within the space of twenty-four hours.

(Preliminary note to *Samson Agonistes.*)

What Milton is advocating, is freedom from convention and a return to the live sources of antiquity (which does not mean that he was not conversant with the theories and works of Western European culture), Homer, Virgil, Holy Scripture, the Greeks just mentioned, as well as Dante, Petrarch, Tasso.

Milton leaves us puzzled. His work seems to transcend 'literature', his scheme is too lofty, the execution too grandiose, for us to apply to him the conventional yard-sticks of romantic, baroque, classical. His epic is more than epic, his tragedy (*Samson Agonistes*) is a meditation, a vast lyric poem rather than a tragedy, and yet in the spirit of the ancients. Clarity of thought and of conception, vast erudition, innumerable allusions to a remote past and the renewed claim that a poem demands active participation by the reader: none of these suffices to categorize the larger-than-life creations of a prophetic mind. The absolute of the classicist is not comparable to Milton's God-centred absolute. And allegory, when all is said, is a medieval mode of thinking, rather than a classical, Mediterranean way of reaching out for the truth! So one must leave it to the individual reader – as always, in the last resort – to append to the writer the label that appears fittest.

4
Renaissance France –
Mairet and sundry matters

There is no need for us to say very much about the exuberant sixteenth century in France. The rapid re-discovery of antiquity and its riches went parallel with the fight against scholasticism; neo-Platonism was in full swing; Petrarch was exerting an undue influence over the French sonneteers. Three powerful magnets attracted the thinkers: traditional Catholicism, Calvinism and, more vaguely, neo-paganism, with its science, its scepticism à la Montaigne, its mythology. Just as important was the fact that new forms of poetry were becoming acclimatized, taken from Greek anthologies and Latin poets and fully exploited, imitated at least, and sometimes well amalgamated. Classicism at its best only appears when the old poetic matter or form has been fully assimilated, fully integrated in the language and vision of the imitator, who then becomes a creator in his own right, the supreme example of this rare process being Jean Racine. When ingestion is complete, the new, grafted on to a sympathetic stem is most likely to grow and to bloom; otherwise the effort proves unavailing. (I am thinking here of Samuel Johnson's tragedy *Irene* and Voltaire's play of the same name.)

It is perhaps to the Renaissance poets that we owe certain misconceptions about the golden ages of Athens and Rome. Not all Greeks were lovers of beauty, men of common sense, perfect citizens, serene and concerned only with the highest and most general concepts. That faraway past was not entirely 'Polis' (city-state) or pastoral. And yet, this glorification of *Hellenism* is part and parcel of our heritage, and has been, for many, a source of inspiration. Man is enamoured of his Utopias, and we find that those situated in the past are more cheerful than those which promise us a 'better' future. More accurately, what has always impressed the lovers of ancient Greece is that sense of proportion, that equilibrium revealed by its temples, statues and writings, that perfect equation of goodness, truth and beauty, which poets like Boileau and Keats tried to recapture. The double precept of teaching and pleasing came naturally to a nation which was perhaps innocent of doubt as we know it, whereas nearly all the modern classicists have felt impelled either to induce pleasure, while merely paying lip service to inculcating moral principles, or vice versa. More deeply yet, man believes, or would like to believe, in what he sees as underlying Greek art and Virgil's poetry, namely *ideal beauty*: perfect equilibrium and harmony, shared by classics and romantics alike. Walter de la Mare called this Platonic ideal:

> A beauty beyond earth's content
> A hope – a half memory.

There may be different ways of approaching it. To quote John Bayley (*The Romantic Survival*), 'Crudely speaking, the criterion of romantic success is to imagine a world different from anyone else's,' and, equally crudely, I might add that the criterion of classic success is to create a world to be shared by all. This is particularly true in seventeenth-century France, where team work was far more marked than in England in any century.

Renaissance in France is characterized by imitation and invention, by its lyrical achievement rather than by its theatre, which was only a sequence of tableaux with long tirades, and by the luxuriance of its often artificially inflated vocabulary. (For a more comprehensive review, consult C. H. Wright's *French Classicism*, Cambridge, 1920.) The civil wars did not impede the flow of literature, a literature that had nevertheless no cohesion, no focal point. When Henry IV of Navarre came to the throne in 1589, he gave France a modicum of stability. His court poet, François de Malherbe (1555–1628), a severe censor of the vocabulary, fought against the verbal excesses of the Pléiade poets and strove to give the French language a corresponding modicum of stability. He stressed the qualities of 'lucidité, volonté, calcul', he insisted on obedience to authority, on purity of style, he set himself up as the arbiter of what was permissible. The rules of prosody are, in his eyes, as strict as those of grammar. 'Malherbe came, and poetry, on seeing him arrive, departed' (Banville, echoing Boileau). Now it is quite possible that Malherbe's efforts and precepts would not have sufficed to give literature a new direction. As it was, another writer, Guez de Balzac (1597–1654), was to do for prose what Malherbe had done for poetry. His innumerable letters were noticed for their polished style and the propriety of their vocabulary. Neatness of turn of phrase, richness of texture and overall planning, these, it might be claimed, came to matter as much as, or even more than, content.

We must look upon Malherbe and Balzac as the forerunners of the great period: the advocates of an intelligible and somehow oratorical verse and prose style, the detractors of the immediate past.

The seventeenth century, we must remember, was as crude and brutal as any other. Nevertheless certain factors were at work which were slowly bringing about changes in people's attitudes: a minimal tolerance shown to splinter-groups, – Huguenots, Free Thinkers – the creation of schools under the Jesuits, the Oratorians and the Jansenists. Charitable institutions were founded for the relief of the sick and the poor, of galley slaves and so on. Just as important, I think, was the civilizing influence of people like Madame de Rambouillet, who assembled noblemen and bourgeois writers and expected of them a certain discipline: better manners, a high degree of politeness, more refined conversation raised to the level of an art. In her salon, psychological topics were discussed, words defined and modern usage elaborated. This gradual refining of the *mores* of the time only affected a minority, but then the whole flowering of literature under Louis XIV remained more or less the concern of a courtly élite. Poets wrote for the king and noble patrons. French literature remained for a long time more *inbred*, less popular in its appeal, than English literature.

L'Astrée (Honoré d'Urfé, 1568–1625), a pastoral romance of immense length, became the romantic 'manuel de la bonne com-pagnie, l'évangile de l'hôtel de Rambouillet' (Boulenger). It is nothing if not escapist literature, a charming fairy tale, which acted upon many minds as an antidote to the trauma of recent wars. I mention it here, merely for its civilizing influence. (Generally speaking, the novel, the modern epic, does not come within the purlieus of this study).

There is no need for us to go into one particular off-shoot of this and other salons: namely *Préciosité*, which, by itself, was only marginally conducive to French classicism. Two genres evolved from games played in the salons: the portrait, and possibly the maxim. Another *romantic* novelist, Madeleine de Scudéry, exempli-fies for us, in *Clélie* and other novels, a number of features typical of the period: platonic tenderness, the frequent use of portraits, and the analysis of terms such as *honnêteté*, *galanterie*, *esprit*, as being the spirit of what is right, fitting, witty, opportune. 'L'air galant de la société consiste principalement à penser les choses d'une manière aisée et naturelle.' At every stage, we see linguistic refinement and limitation successfully waging war on crudity, approximation and enthusiasm. One man was destined to play an important part in eighteenth-century rationalism: René Descartes (1596–1650). Even if the full impact of his system was only to be felt later, this philosopher belongs here, not only because his psychology un-doubtedly influenced Corneille's notion of the magnanimous hero (*le héros généreux*), but because he laid down in his *Discours de la méthode* (see F. Sutcliffe's modern translation) certain principles which informed French classicism, mainly on account of logic and clarity. According to him, there are four main rules for clear thinking:

1. Never accept anything as true until it is patently so (rule of evidence).
2. Divide the subject-matter into as many components as possible (rule of analysis).
3. Proceed from the simple to the complex (rule of synthesis).
4. Revise thoroughly, lest anything be omitted (rule of control).

This discourse was the first serious and successful attempt made at writing philosophy in the vernacular. 'I have written my philosophy in such a way that it can be grasped everywhere, even in Turkey.' Descartes aimed at universality, which is a mark of the classical mind and method, in the same degree as he sought to establish the primacy of reason over imagination (sometimes called, in English, wit or fancy), and in the same manner as he aimed at moral and scientific usefulness. (The seventeenth century produced some magnificent work in the field of physics and mathematics, and one must not be surprised to find a close link between the *rules for thinking* and the *rules for good writing*. Later on, the Royal Society was to exert an undeniable influence on the development of the English language. For further details consult R. F. Jones's 'Science and English Prose Style, 1650–1675' in *Literary English Since Shakespeare*, ed. George Watson, New York, 1970.) To adduce but one example of this thirst for mathematical formulation: it is quite legitimate to see in La Rochefoucauld's *Maxims* a genuine desire to find a single main cause for man's actions, compressed in 'formulae' which should have the rigour of geometrical axioms. The influence of Descartes was subtle and ubiquitous.

'Philosophie de l'enthousiasme contenu,' one critic called it. Keenness and restraint or self-mastery characterize Descartes' method.

Parallel to the gradual change of *temper* of the upper classes, a war was waged between the partisans of Guarini and the partisans of Aristotle. The former, under the leadership of Ogier and others, rebelling against constraint, fought for the triumph of reason over authority (rules) and of tragi-comedy over tragedy; they might be styled *modern*; their contribution to seventeenth-century French literature was relatively slight. We shall meet this opposition again when we discuss briefly the implication of the complex and doubtful notion of the baroque.

The other party found a forceful mouthpiece in the person of Mairet. His preface to *Silvanire* (1631) is a manifesto in defence of classical tragedy; it is also a compromise between respect of the rules, and the demands of reason and common-sense. The reason-rule formula remains rather empty of meaning until we accept that a certain kind of play can be written, for which limiting rules (for example the three unities) will ensure success. To cut a long story short, it is in Mairet's *Sophonisba* (1634), that we must look for the first modern, French, classical tragedy. It is interesting to learn that Mairet borrows his theme from Tressino's *Sophonisbe* (1515), itself modelled on Titus Livius. The debt owed by the French to the Italians was heavy indeed.

Italian-Aristotelian

'Some two years ago, the Cardinal de la Valette and you, you persuaded me to compose a pastoral (*Silvanire*) with the strictness the Italians are accustomed to imposing upon themselves in this pleasant kind of writing . . . The desire I had to please both of you made me study, with great diligence, the works of these great men, in which . . . I finally found that they possessed no greater secret than to take as their yardstick that of the ancients, Greek and Latin, whose rules they observed more religiously than we have done hitherto. And so I proposed to imitate them.' (Mairet)

This passage is typical and could apply to all subsequent upholders of the tradition. The salient point being simply that it was not so much Aristotle as *Aristotle interpreted by the Italians* who called the tune.

The great initiator of the fashion for things Italian was the erudite and lively poet Chapelain. If France was to sing the praises of Italy for quite a few years, Chapelain (1595–1674) was undoubtedly their cheer-leader. His *Letter on the Twenty-Four Hours*, his *Sentiments on the Cid* (in collaboration with others), rest firmly on Castelvetro, Scaliger and so on. By a puzzling consensus of opinion, most critics under the wings of Chapelain taught the same doctrine: unities, decorum, verisimilitude. There may be arguments on points of detail, as well as on the respective superiority of pleasing or teaching as the chief aim of literature, but the doctrine established itself and remained well-nigh unopposed. This success must be attributed at least partly to the dictatorial attitude of Richelieu, minister of Louis XIII, and founder of the Académie Française.

After Chapelain's failure to create an epic masterpiece (*La Pucelle*) the attention of writers was focused on tragedy and comedy. (After Corneille, tragi-comedy died out, and France had to wait for Victor Hugo to take up the challenge, and promote the mixed genre of the Romantic melodrama.)

The Abbé d'Aubignac echoed Chapelain's teaching in his *Pratique du Théâtre* (1657): 'Les règles du théâtre ne sont pas fondées en autorité, mais en raison'. The example of the ancients is followed 'because they use them (the rules) much to their glory. He who wants to become a poet must apply himself to reading Aristotle and Horace ... then he must peruse their commentators ...'. For Jules de la Mesnardière Aristotle is the 'prince of philosophy'. More important than Aristotle idolatry is the general anti-individualistic code imposed on the artist (how crippling this can be will be shown in the eighteenth century), with its rider, according to which knowledge of precept and precedent *makes the poet*. Even if all these keen gentlemen do not quite convince us, we must bear in mind, that no less a genius than Pascal claimed that 'il y a des règles aussi sûres pour plaire que pour démontrer'. Let us bear in mind also, that the climate of opinion thus established led to the creation of exceptionally powerful works. Furthermore, the French theorists shared an opinion which was dear to Descartes, namely that reason, or commonsense, is equally apportioned to all men. Chapelain held that 'Reason is not subject to change'; Balzac that 'It is certain that reason belongs to all nations'; La Mesnardière that 'Reason belongs to all ages'. Art thus placed on the solid pedestal of reason could, at the same time, aim high and remain intelligible. All facets of classicism can be based on this premise. In the words of René Bray, 'Classicism is European. Its cradle is not in France, but it is in France that it received its final shape, that it was organized into a coherent system, that it was consecrated by masterpieces. And classicism is the doctrine of reason. It is also the need for rules; it is admiration for the ancient; it is a preoccupation with utilitarian art . . ., but it is above all, perhaps, the cult of sovereign reason.'

Believing, admiring, imitating, embellishing, generalizing, typifying, probing the mind: activities and attitudes which merge into works we call classical, and in which the ego of the writer hides unflinchingly behind the Ego of Man.

What does one mean by a regular tragedy?
One, undoubtedly, which complies with a set of rules. Unity of action excludes, or at least limits to a minimum, sub-plots and extraneous episodes. Not only should the plot be *simple*, or single-minded, perhaps, but it should be organized so logically that the sequence of events, the actual order of scenes, the series of con-frontations that makes up the play, cannot be altered without

destroying the whole. Then, as the stage itself is limited and as there must be a reasonable relationship between time of action and time of performance, it follows that the action, the story itself, must limit itself to what can happen in reality in a short span of time, say twenty-four hours, as well as in a reduced space, say two distinct yet adjoining places. The number of characters on stage at any time should be kept low. Everything points towards concentration, i.e. the choice, as subject-matter of the play, of a crisis in the life of the hero. According to Goethe's pithy phrase: 'French tragedy is a crisis,' a crisis so momentous that the hero will reveal himself for what he is, shortly before his down-fall. The same need for concentration leads the playwright to cut out ruthlessly anything that is not conducive to that end. Width is sacrificed to depth. (See Racine, Preface to *Mithridate*.)

The crisis can be attributed to a decree of the gods, to fate, to the 'spirit of history': that would be Greek or Senecan. Or motivated and brought about by the very psychology of the hero: that would be French, French since Mairet. In the first case we grieve for the victim, in the second we either admire or loath the hero. In the first case, it is the plot, the historical development, the human predicament that holds our attention; in the second it is psychology and a certain form of nobility which moves us. (Racine's merit lies in his having combined the two types of tragedy considered here into plays of extreme beauty.) Mairet chose, before Corneille and Racine, to alter history (as depicted by ancient historians mainly) for the sake of the play and its credibility. Psychology superseded history: 'je n'ai pas altéré l'histoire sans sujet' (I have not spoiled history without a good reason): the aim being verisimilitude and unity, or impact. Conflicts provide good material for this kind of play, conflicts between love and duty, between two duties, between the individual and the state, between energy and weakness, between reason and feeling. Reduction of the plot to a minimum entails also the need for fairly comprehensive introductory scenes (summary of past events and exposition of the problem to be resolved), for messengers relating off-stage happenings, for mental developments to be conveyed through monologues (which are not mere lamentations or philosophical meditations) and discussions with confidants (all other dialogues being true confrontations). All this may seem too obvious to state, but we must remember that this was not so at the beginning of the seventeenth century. The features of the psychological tragedy grew logically out of each other, but the creation of this kind of writing was no mean achievement. A new model was put before playwrights, to be modified or improved, or to be combined with the looser, traditional kind of tragedy practised by Corneille. The new style established conventions (no character, for example, was to *die* on stage, in full view of the public; that would have been considered unseemly). The classical period more than any other must be understood in terms of conventions, most of them relating either to economy of means or to decorum.

One last point should be made here. Despite its rhetorical approach to language, its rationality and its conventions, the best classical theatre is in no way desiccated: it did not do away with feeling. On the contrary, it acknowledged the mysterious sources of feeling and made use of premonitions, omens and dreams. Irrationality creeps in, subdued.

5
French Classicism: a climax

Before turning to Corneille and further consideration of the complex we call classicism, I wish to return briefly to the notion of stoicism alluded to earlier on, and to draw attention to Basil Willey's *The English Moralists* (1964), in which he discusses the impact made by the Greek philosophical tradition (as modified by the Latins) on the thinkers and poets of the beginning of the modern era. Stoicism, like Platonism, is one of the immortal legacies of antiquity; I say *immortal* because it is, in Willey's own words 'the defensive attitude everywhere taken up by humankind towards outrageous fortune'. Although this is less true in the case of Racine, the classic hero breathes stoicism, he lives and dies stoically, and as most classical tragedies are set in a fairly remote past, he need not be endowed with what Nietzsche would call the virtues of the slave, namely charity and humility. Stoicism means, in effect, self-mastery, a control of the passions that leads to invulnerability and tranquillity of soul. Philosophically speaking, it is an attempt at participating in the changeless, harmonious and rational climate of the cosmos. The seventeenth century rejected the vision, but it kept, by and large, the ethic code underlying stoicism; the stiff upper lip of Epictetus, Marcus Aurelius and Seneca. In this particular scheme of things, the chief faculty of the mind, in its progress upwards, is the will, a rational principle informed by God (or Nature), and the imperative *Follow Nature* was indeed one of the battle cries of the classics. Pushed to extremes, stoicism exudes a cold sternness which Keats called the 'egotistical sublime', a formula applicable to many a Cornelian hero (though, here again, less applicable to the Racinian anti-hero).

The limits of this study do not allow me to linger on the works of Pierre Corneille (1606–1684), who, abroad especially, was held by many to be the most representative of the *grands classiques français*. I shall therefore restrict myself to picking out a few salient points.

Corneille was a versatile writer, whom one cannot easily squeeze into the strait-jacket of a simple definition. His tragedies are of two types: straightforward tragedy and tragi-comedy (with a relatively happy ending). Furthermore, one must clearly distinguish between the creative playwright and the theorist (the author of *préfaces*, *examens* and *discours*). As a theorist, Corneille was indeed an important exponent of the doctrine of classicism: imitation of the ancients; politics as one of the main subjects; a naïve (that is natural) description of virtues and vices; a moral lesson to be taught 'in a delectable way'; an illustrious subject in a remote setting to guarantee verisimilitude; some twisting of history for greater effect; resolution of a crisis; mirroring of an intelligible world; five acts; use of the alexandrine (rhymed couplets, lines of twelve syllables with a more or less rigid break in the middle: antithetical and balanced verse formation). There is to be no chorus, and admiration is aimed at, rather than purgation of passions through fear and pity.

The great tragedies (*Cinna*, *Horace*, *Polyeucte*) prove that Corneille had not only grasped the rules of the psychological tragedy better than anybody else, but also that it was he who brought this art-form, quickly and forcefully, to its first climax. More important to us, however, is the fact – fully realized perhaps only in recent times – that the success of the play mattered much more to Corneille than any kind of regularity. If irregularity gave rise to astonishment and admiration in the spectator, so much the better; Corneille justified his art, but at the same time he felt that there was no need for justification.

I must acknowledge my indebtedness to an eminent critic, E. B. O. Borgerhoff, who in *The Freedom of French Classicism* opened up new vistas on the seventeenth century. It is Mr Borgerhoff's merit to have pointed out, not so much the irrationality of that period, as all that lies behind the rationalism of the *Grand Siècle*: everything which remains so well hidden in the mysterious little phrase 'un certain je ne sais quoi'. (For an interesting contrast, one should read Bénichou's chapter on Corneille in *Morales du grand siècle*.)

In his work as a whole, written over a very long period, Corneille appears much less of a classic than the textbooks had given us to understand, despite the protestations of faith in the doctrine, despite the many appurtenances of the genre and despite the grand manner and the sententious style. He now stands before us as a very independent mind, as an artist who sounds out public opinion and panders to its taste for strong emotions, an overgrown child who still believes in magic and make-believe: 'the ingenious weaving of fiction (and what fiction in the comedies especially!) with truth, wherein consists the most beautiful secret of poetry', said Corneille himself. Which is the true Corneille: the classic? the romanesque? the *dreamer* (as in *Suréna*, his last, most Racinian, elegiac tragedy)? the mephistophelian, whose characters sometimes seem to rise above the distinction between good and evil? the believer who laboured for years over a verse-translation of the *Imitation*? the pragmatist? (Borgerhoff applies this last term to Corneille the man. I wonder whether there is not in the plays themselves, in *Rodogune* particularly, a *démarche* of the hero, a way of progressing, which is hesitant and groping, made up of waiting for circumstances to dictate the next step. It might be claimed that the real hero of much of this theatre is life itself, which would perhaps go a certain way towards explaining the impact Corneille made outside his own country, especially in England.)

Each writer has his own method; I do not blame other people's, and I stick to mine . . . one's judgement is free in these matters, and tastes vary.

(Preface to *Héraclius*.)

His heroes are at one and the same time self-movers and the toys of life. (For Corneille's theoretical writings, see *Writings on the Theatre, Préfaces, Examens and Discours*, edited by H. Barnwell, Blackwell 1965.)

By the time Corneille gave his *Nicomède* in 1651, the first phase of French classicism was over. A first climax had been reached. The Fronde, the mid-century civil war, had ended with the defeat of the nobility and the parliamentarians; Mazarin's rule was well-nigh absolute and soon the King was to take the reins of the state into his own firm hands, and France was to become, for quite some time, not only the most highly populated and most powerful nation in Europe, but also the most influential. Louis XIV had one aim: the greatness of France and the glorification of its king. The whole nation felt inspired or compelled to work towards that aim, which was set high; the King demanded perfection. The loftiness of his plans is reflected in the paintings of the time, in the furniture produced, in the parks laid out by Le Nôtre, in breathtaking buildings such as Versailles. France experienced something new: a sense of urgency in creating beauty on a large scale: team-work was essential. What is particularly interesting is that, in spite of the 'common goal' and the formalism imposed by the Sun King on all, the great writers of the day did not feel under any particular compulsion; as long as they gave a little better than their best, they were free to work as they wished. Their achievements finally surpassed those of the other artists. It is to them that we turn for grandeur *and* spirit, for intuition *and* perfect formulation. In French classicism a nation discovered a way to express itself.

Many genres found, as if by miracle, their greatest representatives: Pascal, La Rochefoucauld, Molière, Racine, Mme de

Sévigné, Mme de La Fayette, Boileau, La Bruyère, Bossuet: all urged on by the King's pleasure, and supported by a relatively small society of amateurs and connoisseurs. An élite-literature, bearing witness to a privileged moment of French history, classical on account of many of its finest features.

For present purposes, a few reminders must suffice. In Pascal's *Provinciales* French prose reached one of its early summits. Pascal had mastered the art of blending irony with urbanity, concision and clarity with completeness and flawless logic. Mme de Sévigné's letters to her daughters are a model of polished correspondence. Molière, in the psychological comedy, remains unsurpassed. He was in no way a pariah of classicism, as Victor Hugo once claimed. He saw that the so-called Aristotelian rules were only a means to an end, the end being above all to please. (For the psychology of laughter and some of the reasons why comedy can exert a moral influence, see Bergson's *Le Rire*.) Most striking here is the absence of models for many of the plays, especially those castigating hypocrisy, vices, privileges, etc. One should not exaggerate the moralizing intentions of the French classical writers. After all, they were successful, and we turn to them because they are moving, or interesting, that is, deeply satisfying and beautiful. We do not owe all our self-knowledge to Freud or Gestalt-psychologists. The seventeenth century has much to teach us about our passions (even if we hardly us the word nowadays), or *amour-propre* (even if it is repugnant to us!). Which other century of literature has ever been quite so successful at generalizing its findings in terms of important human types? Stressing what matters, categorizing without pedantry, impressing and convincing by letting knowledge and beauty grow out of each other: these are some of the hall-marks of classicism at its best, classicism that somehow transcends itself.

The *Misanthrope* demonstrates how far this quest for beauty can go, how near it takes us to the more modern concept of art for art's sake: a play made of apparently nothing, a stirring ballet leading nowhere; so remote and yet so immediate, somewhere between absolute truth and absolute illusion. Quite typical, too, of this period is Molière's incessant war against eccentricity, eccentricity being an infringement of the rules dictated by common sense and *honnêteté* (the most ubiquitous and least definable word of the century). Molière was asking for more freedom within the bounds of a society at the same time more reasonable and more flexible.

La Fontaine I must mention at least in passing. He chose to compose mainly fables, a genre which allowed great freedom of expression, since the doctrine did not prescribe any particular rules for it. His vocabulary was rich for the period, and he used it to such effect that, especially in the later fables, he reached the summit of his art, and wrote some of the most impressive French ever written.

Whereas La Fontaine hovered lightly above the more controlled classicism of his contemporaries, Mme de la Fayette created within its framework a new genre, the psychological novel. Legislation there was none concerning novels, which thus afforded much latitude for experimentation. *La Princesse de Clèves* (1678) was to the novel what Mairet's *Sophonisbe* had been to the tragedy. In *La Littérature Française du Siècle Classique* (Paris, 1943), V. L. Saulnier has this semi-complimentary comment to make: 'The skill of psychological analysis and delicacy of expression give this book its value, thanks to which the author continued to enjoy a discreet notoriety.' (For Dryden's comments I refer the reader to N. Lee's exploitation of the theme of the *Princess of Cleves*, to the epilogue in particular!) Striking in this novel are the economy of means and the total lack of local colour. Everything, excepting the feelings of the characters, is beautifully open and generalized: one is reminded of Claude Lorrain's classical landscapes and La Rochefoucauld's amazing power of concentration.

Racine's contribution to literature cannot be assessed in a few lines. The three-dimensional world of his plays (written between 1667 and 1691), their deceptive simplicity, the absence of metaphors, all heighten the 'majestic sadness' Racine achieved by the purely psychological motivation, the crystallization of a past culture and a linguistic heritage by one who claimed that, 'The whole of invention consists in making something out of nothing', the clarity in speech and self-awareness, the resignation and the 'harmonizing of unsettled states of mind', the interplay of feelings having a universal validity: none of these features can be made to fit into the pattern of a school, even a movement as impressive as modern classicism.

The rules and all possible restraints suited Racine's purpose: they simply provided a base for his quest for beauty and truth about man. He incarnates the spirit of all that is best about classicism, he brings it in a few years to an unsurpassed peak. He had no successors worthy of the name except for Goethe, who only followed him after many changes had been wrought on the literary climate of Europe. (See in particular Eugène Vinaver, *Racine et la Poésie Tragique* (Paris, 1951), O. de Mourgues, *Racine or the Triumph of Relevance* (Cambridge University Press, 1967).)

Before considering La Rochefoucauld's important contribution to classicism, I must stop briefly at his less typical successor as a moralist, La Bruyère. Jean de la Bruyère stands a trifle forlorn at the end of the century, half classical with his yearning for stability (behind the Church, the King and the Ancients), half modern with his tinge of relativism and his pointillistic mode of writing. For him, we feel, the world was still fully intelligible; it sufficed to focus one's attention on appearances to reach the real self. The *mask* presented no real difficulty for the creator of the *Characters* (definitive edition, 1694). But we recognize in him modern traits: art being its own justification, or feeling slowly superseding reason as the main source of conviction. He just about succeeded in keeping straight the balance between new and old, between feeling and reason, between the individual and the social being. (See L. van Delft, *La Bruyère Moraliste*, Droz, 1971.)

Of all the literary genres, it is possibly the maxim that requires the highest degree of concentration. La Rochefoucauld's collection (definitive edition, 1678) surpasses anything done before or after him. Classical in this influential work are its unity of tone, the subservience of each part to the whole, the uncompromising seriousness of La Rochefoucauld's intent (notwithstanding irony, which is the safety-valve of classicism). In the maxims, the writer discovered a way of probing the mind by means of a quasi-mathematical (and yet at times poetically suggestive) formula, and of expressing one of the commonplaces of the seventeenth century, namely that, unless regenerated by grace, man is motivated by an abysmal selfishness (self-love, *amour-propre*). I use the epithet *abysmal* quite deliberately. The *Maximes* seem to draw heavily on an early piece of writing (known as Max. 563) which can be regarded as an extraordinary intuition of what we now call the unconscious. The notion of the unconscious, however, does not fit readily into the pattern of classicism: it is connected with that substratum coyly called 'un certain je ne sais quoi'. (Rapin and Bouhours, representative of 'all that is tiresome and naïvely arrogant of Seventeenth-Century French classicism', Borgerhoff shows clearly as having been fully aware that art has *secret graces and hidden beauties known by very few people, mysteries incompre-hensible to the human mind*.) Maxime 563 consists, if we do not look too closely at the punctuation, of a single three page sentence, the stylistic features of which are not classical at all. There is a tension there, an uncontrolled vivacity, a certain imagery which seem to belong to another world, to another kind of sensitivity, not subjectively romantic, not modelled either on popular thought, yet sophisticated and powerful.

We are up against something which, as I have just said, does not fit snugly into the framework of classicism, a theme and style to

which some historians of literature have appended, rather con-
fusingly, the label of *romanticism*, and others the as yet ill-defined
label of *baroque*. Baroque at first denoted the ornate style of
Counter-Reformation architecture and ornamentation, which had
spread from Spain to Austria. Art critics, in Germany particularly,
found that the sometimes bizarre, often over-wrought, features of
this style matched the manner and conception of writings of the late
Renaissance and the first half of the seventeenth century. Soon the
critics of other countries began to talk about baroque periods,
schools and sub-styles. The definitions varied greatly and became
more and more comprehensive. Those interested will find a survey
of the history and implications of the term in Wellek's *Concepts
of Criticism*. What concerns us here is the baroque as one of the
limits of classicism and as a constant source of interference with it.
It would be quite feasible to write a history of English or French
literature without once using this relatively new-fangled word.
But as an alternative to *romantic* it is not to be dismissed lightly.

Baroque denotes strangeness, tension, irrationality, eccentricity
and the grotesque. It denotes an art that is lavish in its thoughts
and means, which aims at surprise and luxuriance, which shuns no
hyperbole (while classical art cherishes the litotes). It does not
know any rules but those it imposes upon itself. Wellek quotes
from a fascinating book by Jean Rousset (*La Littérature de l'Age
Baroque*, Paris, 1954) who studies some of the concepts underlying
baroque writing: the instability of the world, its dream-like quality
(the world is as a stage), the theme of metamorphosis, i.e. the
protean character of life, the preponderance of masks and disguises,
the theme of the mirror, the need to shine and to show off. Life is
seen as a carousel, a ballet, a sham. The metaphors of the poets,
by growing unintelligible, emphasize its opacity. In the meantime
Rousset has reassessed his ideas (in *L'Intérieur et L'Extérieur*,
Paris, 1968). Maybe his first book covered too much material,
went too far in its conclusions; there were, after all, works which,

although not classical, were less extreme than others in their baroquism: merely mannered, such as those of the Marinists, the Gongorists, belated Euphuists, metaphysical poets, précieux and others. Moreover, there were baroque elements in the classical writers and in the more sugary rococo of the eighteenth century.

The baroque, for better or worse, must stand for that vein which emerged quite regularly (making up so much of Corneille's charm for example) all through the century, and went underground, so to speak, only in the heyday of classicism. The rationalism of the classics and of the Enlightenment held it back somehow, until it emerged again during what is called pre-romanticism, when it began to acquire a further characteristic, namely, the solipsism of the romantic poet-hero. (The classical hero is a social being: he must be seen to be a hero.) Imagination, more or less controlled, is the hall-mark of the baroque. It sets no store by authority, rule, reason, or photographic realism.

Literature does not progress in neat stages; all basic attitudes manifest themselves more or less simultaneously, one having usually the upper hand at any given period. It is therefore not surprising to see classical works enriched or marred by baroque elements. To put it differently, classicism is one of those periodic attempts at putting one's emotional house in order. Stylistically, the progress can be assessed in the passage from the long reflection on *amour-propre* to the mature *maxime*, or from the first draft of La Rochefoucauld's *Mémoires* to the revised version with its marked binary rhythm.

The French classic most often quoted by the English Augustan poets was probably Boileau. Nicolas Boileau (1636–1711) contributed greatly to shaping French classicism and he summed it up in his famous *Art Poétique*. We still read his satirical *Lutrin* (The Lectern), his Horatian *Epistles* and his Juvenalian *Satires*, but he owed his fame and his influence on English and German literature mainly to his theoretical work and to his translation of and commentary on Longinus' treatise on the sublime. His didacticism rather than his original compositions was partly responsible for the survival of classicism in the eighteenth century and, who knows, for the dearth of poetry in France until the advent of André Chénier. It was as if ossification set in as soon as the Universities started *teaching* Boileau.

For him there is nothing between the worst and the best in literature. At heart he was a perfectionist and an enthusiast, and not, as was believed for a long time, a pedantic schoolmaster. His many attacks against mediocrity were undertaken in the name of absolute beauty, which has little to do with imitation and arbitrary rules. His belief in genius, untypical of classicism, contributed to making him palatable to English poets, even though they tended to look upon him merely as the mouthpiece of Aristotle. 'Merveille' and 'beau désordre' he preached as much as regularity and reason. Reason is not in any way deified; it remained for him at the level of spirited common sense. How scathing he can wax against the 'poètes plats', the pedestrian mind! Anything capable of moving mind and heart found favour with Boileau – within reason and the limits of decorum. (For a brief assessment see Nathan Edelman, *L'Art Poétique*, reproduced in a highly useful anthology of critical essays: *French Classicism*, ed. Jules Brody.)

6

Restoration and Augustan Classicism

Literature can be likened to a strong rope which, at any point, will reveal to the static onlooker but one strand squarely, others fading, and yet others appearing. At each point of time, one vein will stand out, one movement overshadow the others. Optimism or pessimism, progress or reaction, extravagance or control; social or personal, baroque or realistic, romantic or classical. All strands and attitudes inseparably entwined, though achieving prominence in turn, thanks to an individual, a school of thought, a fad maybe or a strong ruler. French classicism had its peak between 1660 and 1680 and centred on Louis xiv and Jean Racine, supported by a Corneille, a Pascal, a La Rochefoucauld, a Bossuet (the champion of Catholic orthodoxy), a Boileau (not to mention a host of theorists, artists, decorators, gardeners and men of political and military genius). When we turn to Restoration England, we find no such uniformity of purpose, no focal point, in other words no favourable ground for such a movement.

English writers, picking up the threads after Cromwell's regime, on the return of the King from France, slipped quite easily back into the traditional mould. The Court had indeed imported certain foreign habits, refinements in speech and dress, and French theories presented a challenge to poets who took it up half-heartedly. Most playwrights borrowed French themes, but hardly the spirit underlying them: the plumes, not the heart. They quite deliberately pandered to the taste of the public for drama, blood and thunder, irregularity and mixed genres. (Shadwell's attempts at *improving* on Shakespeare and Molière are truly pathetic.) The merits of Restoration comedy have little to do with classicism, whatever the definition one might give. The English way of writing has always been freer and more pragmatic in its approach to life, history and art.

Any earlier attempts at a *closed* form (as opposed to the open Shakespearean one), such as Samuel Daniel's *Cleopatra*, seem to have led merely to exoticism, romance and intricacy. Chapman, strongly Senecan, had stressed one of the few classical dogmas that made a lasting impact, namely the moral purpose, in accord with the religious temper of the times. The Italian theorists never gained the authority they had enjoyed on the other side of the Channel, nor did love of authority extend to foreign imports, models or theories. And if Ben Jonson is called the classic English playwright, it is because of his Latinity, his grasp of Roman power-politics, his Horatian irony, rather because he offers a closed world picture or closed form. His example of a half-way classicism did not suffice to lead to a real rapprochement: classicism *à la française* was effectively blocked by the English temperament, by a different tradition, and possibly by a new, scientific, spirit.

In the last resort, the classical conventions and the Elizabethan heritage proved incompatible and, as long as playwrights such as Dryden insisted on compromises, no great plays were to appear. Furthermore, no English writer was, I believe, prepared to subject his language to the cuts which, at that time, led to the paucity of vocabulary and the concentration and stylization of Racine's art. In France, decorum played havoc with the language, thus excluding vast sources of metaphors and much raciness, and finally bringing poetry to a state of lethargy. Racine and convention somehow exhausted poetic utterance, as Shakespeare had not done. Corneille avoided the trap up to a point, diversified his efforts and thus remained more accessible to English readers.

To assess the relative classicism of creative artists is arduous enough, but as soon as one enters the world of the critics, of the poet-critics, the picture grows even more confused. The lack of clearly defined critical terms made them all talk at cross purposes. What was meant by Nature, by Reason, by Art? Leaving Flecknoe and Rymer aside (*A Short Discourse of the English Stage* and *The Tragedies of the Last Age* respectively), I intend to ask where Dryden really stood.

Dryden was the 'father of English criticism', the great versatile writer of the Restoration, the enthusiastic experimenter with the heroic couplet, the elegant translator of Virgil, Juvenal, Persius, Horace, Ovid, Theocritus, the magnificent satirist, the modern prose stylist, the seeker after order (like his French contemporary La Bruyère): the *amateur* in the best sense of the word.

Very much aware of what went on around him and yet completely immersed in the world of the Romans, he squandered much of his talent by scattering it. And one of the avenues he pursued was the French classical one, Rapin's and Corneille's. He digested imperfectly and imparted ambiguously what he found there. The epilogue to the after all non-classical, rhetorical, bombastic, ironical, sensuous and unconvincing *Aureng-Zebe* shows him, as so often, on the fence. The rules are all right, he seems to say, but the English public wants meat, not 'Monsieur's paltry art'. 'Our Poet writes a hundred years too soon.' This line may contain one of the clues to our understanding of Dryden's position: little does he care about Corneille and art from across the Channel! What does matter, on the contrary, is the civilizing influence of himself and others, on a country which is ready for the headier form of art, at a time when it was becoming more and more aware of vast scientific changes in man's vision of the world. Despite his successes (for he was a *successful* writer of comedies and dramas), and despite the lasting value of many of his poems and famous *purple passages*, his merit seems to lie in the technical field and in his Virgil translation, a model of the genre. To sum up, classicism was for him but a temptation. He was perhaps a poet's poet. (See

John Dryden, *An Essay of Dramatic Poesy* (1668) in *English Classical Essays XVI-XVIII Centuries*, O.U.P.)

As far as Dryden enters into this study, we find on the side of *classicism*: a deep-seated need for order, love of the ancients, acquaintance with the rules and writings of the French, compact expression in general and balanced statements, in a much improved heroic couplet, a sharp sense of antithesis (with its classical binary rhythm), a rudimentary form of transposition (for he did at least paint an idealized picture of reality), a large stock of mythological and pagan relics, rationality and much elegance, and very little confessional poetry. On the side of the *modern*: interest in science, flirtation with Hobbes' materialism, uncertainty, versatility, patriotism, a taste for romantic plots, earthy raciness, a liking for mixed genres (baroque features), the impossibility for him of relinquishing his cultural heritage, a view of the world which is neither static nor tragic, but forward-looking, accepting change, stressing the dynamics of the individual. (For appreciation see also G. Watson's *The Literary Critics*, and G. Steiner's *The Death of Tragedy*.)

Dryden fluctuated between exuberance and restraint, between coarseness and refinement. All through his writing he paid lip-service to the doctrine of decorum, but it is, after all, the Dryden of the 1690s, who, combining the familiar with the reflective, gave his successors models of harmony as well as of much improved satire. It is the blending of realism and eloquence, of experience and commentary, which make him the first Augustan. To the clarity of prose of his *Essay*, he added the clarity of a poetry which owed as much to Ovid, Horace and Virgil as to Chaucer. There is little justification for talking about a French influence.

After reading *Polyeucte*, *Phèdre*, *Le Misanthrope*, a 'maxime', a 'portrait', or one of La Fontaine's philosophical fables, one feels strongly tempted to compare a French masterpiece to a beautiful painting which is *'framed'*, which stands out strongly against its background, aloof and detached, weaned from its author, transcending time, linked mainly by echoes and psychology to history and life. Art supersedes blunt reality and the moral lesson: it is, at one and the same time, stylized and convincing. The works just mentioned, Boileau's too and Bossuet's, all adhere to the spirit of the rules, but not to the letter.

Their authors each brought a genre to its perfection (as incidentally Dryden did for the dignified heroic satire in *Absalom and Achitophel*). They did not do away with the mystery of life, they delved into it, keeping over it that extraordinary control, which marks the true classical period of French literature. Whatever they had to say, after they had left behind a certain down-to-earthness (which Dryden hardly ever abandoned), was matched by a form, in the full sense of the word, which to them, I feel, mattered as much as the subject of their work. I wonder who was wiser? – Dryden and the Augustans with their insistence on the poet's moralizing mission, or the French classicists whose lessons lie dormant in their works, as if pleasing was the poet's calling.

Dryden was the pioneer, Pope his beneficiary.

To read Pope well is to read him again, after putting to one side the doctrine (*Essay on Criticism*), the philosophy (*Essay on Man*), the translations and imitations as such (Homer, Virgil, Ovid, Horace), the vindictiveness of satire (*The Dunciad*, the *Epistles*), the stance of the man of letters, with his moral commonplaces and didacticism. Pope's was an assimilative mind: see, grasp, remember, exploit, condense and impart (to a small group of kindred spirits who did not miss a single reference). This amounts to a great deal already, but, to put it briefly, Pope transcends his framework and method in various ways:

a. He would admit, with Quintilian and others, that beauty rises above precepts, that poetry cannot be taught: artistic creation is not merely an intellectual activity.

b. That imitation (of an Ovidian landscape, for example) must never exclude the present, the objects and sensibilities of one's time.

c. That, ideally, the conventions adopted are no substitute for one's own poetic temperament (nervous and elegiac in the *Pastorals*). The satires I regard partly as a compromise solution: hyper-sensitivity, frustrated by a scheme of things too narrow, turns into skilfully formulated vindictiveness.

d. The detail of each fragment of poem is organized along two different lines: either towards the *sentence*, the *maxim*, without double meaning or poetic resonance – *univox* verse which is highly organized prose; or towards a perfect blending together of statement, reminiscence, mood, imagery. There, Pope's dexterity goes beyond skill; there, his inventiveness and speed, as he passes from one idea to another, are truly surprising. There lastly, we have classicism reaching above itself. Very often, Pope comes into his own, and he enjoys it. He plays with words better than any of his contemporaries. The *classic* gives way to *homo ludens*. This *homo ludens* is not a joker, but a creator of form: he *in-forms* the tragedy of Racine and the *Misanthrope*. He combines sensitivity and intuition with the pure intellect and its attendant *verbum*.

Pope remains the supreme Augustan classic, because he was an impure classic.

Two cant words in modern criticism are 'romantic' and 'classical' – cant words, I borrow his own phrase (Samuel Johnson's); but he did not apply it to them, for he did not recognize the distinction implied in these handy labels which may save the trouble of clear thinking. I should like to have heard him giving his views on these two words, so dear to critics for the last hundred years. Some of us today are far from sure what they mean. But assuming for the moment that there is a clear distinction between the 'classical' and the 'romantic', that

impersonality is the prerogative of the one, and that the other takes under its wing the more intimate individual experiences with their evanescent shades of feeling, we shall then have to say that Johnson wrote his 'romantic' poems in Latin and his 'classical' poems in English. By any definition of the term that I know, some of his Latin poems are 'romantic'. But it is a term of which I wish that we were rid.
(D. N. Smith, *Johnson's Poems*, in *Samuel Johnson, A Collection of Critical Essays*, 'Twentieth Century Views', 1965)

Johnson's marked (Augustan or classical) preference for the rhymed couplet over blank verse (except for Milton's which he appreciated) is significant of that perfect balance between intellect and emotion D. N. Smith detects in his mature work, after he had learnt to control the 'extatick fury' of his earliest poems. Since Dryden, according to Johnson, 'English poetry had no tendency to relapse to its former savageness'. A sign of the taming of the beast was to be afforded by the use of words not 'too familiar, or too remote', of a middle-of-the-road diction. In 'Johnson the Critic', F. R. Leavis puts it like this: 'Johnson's sense of "music" carries with it inseparably a demand for the social movement and tone so characteristic of Augustan verse, and the demand for these is an implicit introduction of the associated norms, rational and moral.' Norms mean truth,

> If truths like these with pleasing language join:
> > (*Prologue* to *Irene*)

they mean rules of life as well as literary themes, and standards for literary criticism: sincerity above all, then integrity, simplicity, resignation, dignity (of poetry, or of one who retires after having led a useful life), utility and finally detachment. The Augustan scheme and Johnson's ideas were nothing if not coherent.

This close connection between the world of letters, the conventions of poetry, and the professed morality of the age gives a cumulative power to the best Augustan verse. It seems to belong to a complete civilisation, and to provide a coherent philosophy of existence – unadventurous, unmysterious . . . , but authoritative, realistic, and instinct with dignity.

(R. Trickett, *The Honest Muse*, Oxford, 1967)

This portrait of the age, applicable to Samuel Johnson, is enhanced by his preference for the general over the particular, the normative over the exploratory. Neither a mystic nor a solitary – thus basically a social being with a sense of urgency, to whom, in the face of death, happiness counted for little (in heroic classicism happiness is the possible outcome of willpower exercised) – Johnson needed to express clearly unequivocal thoughts, beside which there is no other set of *poetical* truths. Augustan classicism was more bourgeois in spirit and possibly in language – peaceful epithets creating the mood, unless satire was aimed at, to castigate vice and deviant behaviour – than its French counterpart in the seventeenth century (yet fairly similar to French neo-classicism in the age of Voltaire).

Two quotations will help us to sum up the doctrine: one concerning *Lycidas*: 'In the poem, there is no nature, for there is no truth'; and in the *Prologue to Irene*:

> In Reason, Nature, Truth, he dares to trust:
> Ye Fops, be silent, and yet Wits, be just![1]

Johnson's poetry was, inevitably, a poetry of statement; this, and the fact that he did not have a dramatic cast of mind, hardly

[1] The self-deprecatory, sometimes even farcical tone of many Augustan prologues and epilogues calls for comment in passing; they may be witty, but they often jar. Many of the plays are either stilted or so unsophisticated that the reader does not feel far removed from the school-play or the pantomime, or, as Bonamy Dobree puts it in *Restoration Tragedy* (Oxford, 1929): 'the boulevard successes of Henri Bernstein are the progeny, after several generations, of *Sophonisba* (Nat Lee) and *The Conquest of Granada* (Dryden)'. Even serious works are sometimes marred by prologues and epilogues which remind one, like the worst plays themselves, of the French Grand-Guignol, to borrow once more from Dobree. Decorum was perhaps only skin-deep . . .

allowed him to come to terms satisfactorily with Shakespeare or the metaphysical poets. Johnson was perhaps afraid of delving too far under the surface of life (or he thought it irrelevant) and of looking too closely at its detailed manifestations: 'Great thoughts are always general, and consist in positions not limited by exceptions, and in descriptions not descending to minuteness.'

At one with Augustan society which formed him and which he repaid with interest, Johnson appears to have been its last true representative. However, modern critics have attempted to show that he was also something of an iconoclast: he would have nothing to do with the famous three unities, or with the all-pervading idea of the Great Chain of Being extolled by the neo-stoics; he was a precursor, moreover, not only of modern lexicography, but also of Sainte-Beuve and his biographical approach to literary criticism, and anticipated 'Wordsworth in one place and Shelley in another' (for details see H. W. Donner, *Dr. Johnson as Literary Critic*, in the above anthology); and, more tellingly perhaps, his psychology, as applied in the *Rambler*, was far ahead of his time, when he propounded ideas such as the *strata* of the mind, 'the role of fantasy, the function of repression, the desire to forget, the wish to avoid reality' (see K. M. Grange, *S. Johnson's Account of Certain Psychoanalytic Concepts*, in the above anthology), where we recognize some of the key-elements of Freudian psycho-analysis. (We find the same kind of intuition in Reynolds' diagnosis of Johnson's pathological condition as a guilt-complex, reported by Boswell.)

Before passing on to a brief comparison of Johnson's tragedy *Irene* with Voltaire's, I should like to quote Johnson's interpretation of catharsis (again reported by Boswell):

Why, Sir, you are to consider what is the meaning of purging in the original sense. It is to expel impurities from the human body. The mind is subject to the same imperfection. The passions are the great movers of human actions; but they are mixed with such impurities, that it is necessary they should be purged or refined by means of terror and pity. For instance, ambition is a noble passion; but by seeing upon the stage, that a man who is so excessively ambitious as to raise himself by injustice, is punished, we are terrified at the fatal consequences of such a passion. In the same manner a certain degree of resentment is necessary; but if we see that a man carries it too far, we pity the object of it, and are taught to moderate that passion. (My record upon this occasion does great injustice to Johnson's expression, which was so forcible and brilliant, that Mr. Cradock whispered to me, 'O that his words were written in a book!')

Written forty years apart, *Irene* and *Irène* can quite usefully be read in conjunction. These tragedies, neither typical of the human condition, were composed by the most representative writers of their period, Johnson and Voltaire (no love lost between them, but points of contact existed, which belong to the study of rationalism rather than of classicism). Hardly anybody reads these two middle-eastern dramas nowadays, and yet they are typical, both moving, and rather artificial; Johnson's is more elegiac, Voltaire's more philosophical.

Irene is loosely constructed, and the motivation at each step of the development remains rudimentary. On reading scene after scene, on reflecting on the impact made, one realizes that what is actually unfolding is a story in dialogue form, where chance leads the characters to and fro: Aspasia, steadfast in her faith, to safety; the unfortunate and wavering Irene, to her doom. Virtue, hardly tested, finds its reward, whereas weakness is punished beyond reason. Garrick was perhaps right when he said: 'When Johnson writes tragedy, declamation roars, and passion sleeps: when Shakespeare wrote, he dipped his pen in his own heart.' The declamation is there indeed, and the tiresome personifications, and the cancerous adjectives, but these faults do not succeed in drowning the occasional music floating above the din of plot and counter-plot.

That wealth, too sacred for their country's use!
That wealth, too pleasing to be lost for freedom!
That wealth, which, granted to their weeping prince,
Had rang'd embattled nations at our gates!
But, thus reserv'd to lure the wolves of Turkey,
Adds shame to grief, and infamy to ruin.
Lamenting Av'rice now too late discovers
Her own neglected in the publick safety . . .

suddenly soars above itself and sings:

Tomorrow's action! Can that hoary wisdom,
Born down with years, still doat upon to-morrow!
That fatal mistress of the young, the lazy,
The coward, and the fool, condemn'd to lose
An useless life in waiting for to-morrow,
To gaze with longing eyes upon to-morrow,
Till interposing death destroys the prospect!
Strange! that this gen'ral fraud from day to day
Should fill the world with wretches undetected
. . . .
To-morrow brings the visionary bride.
But though, too old to bear another cheat,
Learn, that the present hour alone is man's.

This is as yet more tentative than the lines from *The Vanity of Human Wishes* so much praised by T. S. Eliot; but we can hear some of that '*minimal* quality of poetry', whose proximity to prose Eliot found so satisfying. This poetry has a charm of its own – once the reader has rid himself of certain modern preconceptions – and it is Augustan. The full dissociation of poetry from prose had not yet taken place; writing still hinged on concepts which 'were based ultimately on an acceptance of the homogeneity of all discourse as the means by which man, as a rational being, could know and control the universe he lived in' (K. G. Hamilton, *The Two Harmonies*, Oxford, 1963). But the parting was at hand: personal emotion, word-patterns, imagery, etc., were already

E

gaining a modicum of independence, visibly so in Gray and Goldsmith, two transitional poets.

'Blank verse', wrote Voltaire, in 1778, 'was the invention of sloth and the inability to rhyme, as the famous Pope has told me twenty times. To insert in a tragedy, whole scenes in prose is to avow an even more shameful lack of power.' *Irene* is in blank verse, often monotonous, yet not as monotonous as Voltaire's over-regular alexandrines. *Irène* observes the rules, it is based on the principle of crescendo, the later confrontations being fiercer than the earlier ones, it runs its course with the inevitability and resonances of a hundred stock tragedies: all very lofty, precise, expressed in language desiccated by winds that had blown across the French stage for nearly two hundred years already. Each step carries an echo of the past, and it is not until the end, when the thesis appears (intolerance and bigotry have killed the steadfast *Irène*, trapped between duty (= father) and love (= emperor), that attention is drawn, not to art, but to an *idea*, to the personal conviction of the now fully awakened playwright.

Irène presents an ossified structure whereas *Irene* seems to have held a promise for the future. True Augustan poetry needed no *saving*, whereas eighteenth-century French classicism was doomed to die, although it proved so strong that the romantic movement never succeeded completely in bringing about its downfall.

7
Some theory

It is legitimate to speak of a classical or neo-classical period in English literature: legitimate mainly because of a consensus of opinion among poets, whatever their idiosyncrasies and whatever the merits of their respective creative work. Students of the period will benefit greatly from Irène Simon's *Neo-Classical Criticism, 1660–1800*. She has succeeded in presenting in a particularly lucid and attractive way, all the salient points of the doctrine underlying the said consensus of critical opinion. I hope that my present summary will inspire others to go to her for her general introduction and for the extremely appropriate quotations that go to make up the bulk of her book.

'I never heard of any other foundation of dramatic poesy than the imitation of nature; . . . if nature has to be imitated, then there is a rule for imitating nature rightly.' 'The one main end of nature is to please, and imitation pleases.' We can imitate nature 'for nature is still the same in all ages' (Dryden). John Dennis, (*The Grounds of Criticism in Poetry*, 1704) agrees and enlarges:

> if the end of poetry be to instruct and reform the world, that is to bring mankind from irregularity, extravagance, and confusion, to rule and order, how this should be done by a thing that is in itself irregular and extravagant, is difficult to be conceived. Besides the work of every reasonable creature must derive its beauty from regularity; for reason is rule and order. . . . Now the works of God, though infinitely various, are extremely regular.

Besides, 'there is for poetry, no system of known rules but those which are in Aristotle and his interpreters'.

Thomas Rymer (*Tragedies of the Last Age*, 1677) and William

Temple (*Of Poetry*, 1690), among others, insist on the 'moral lesson' (moderating violent passion, correcting ill customs, and so on). Richard Hurd was to repeat these precepts as late as 1766 in his *Dissertation of the Idea of Universal Poetry*; so, too, did Robert Lowth, who in 1787 emphasized *Utility* as the *ultimate object*. Thus the ends are clear, even though the proposed methods differ. They go from terror to castigation, through satire, from pleasure to increased happiness, and through happiness to virtue. The common source is the Horatian tag, 'A poet should instruct or please or both' (depending perhaps on the degree of Puritanism informing the temper of each critic or poet).

No theorist of classicism has ever convincingly explained what *imitation of nature*, one of the main tenets of the doctrine, really meant. If there is any agreement at all, it may be this: take from what you know to be right, what you think will please and instruct. Keep your imitation either to general principles or to telling details (a miser will be a miser *all the time*). There is therefore a close connection between the theory of imitation and the classical art of typifying, of drawing *characters*, of castigating a vice (rather than an individual). People and modes of behaviour can be classified and understood. Nature here again holds no mysteries and poetry moves within a rather more shallow zone than the baroque or the romantic: less craggy, of a more controlled flight, gentler, as in the landscapes of Lorrain. Imitated nature is somehow tamed and stylized by a need for clarity.

> First follow NATURE, and your judgement frame
> By her just standard, which is still the same:
> *Unerring Nature*, still divinely bright,
> One *clear*, *unchang'd* and *universal* light,
> Life, force, and beauty, must to all impart,
> At once the *source*, and end, and *test of art*.

Thus the tone and the matter, in Pope's inimitable way of blending thought and form, which somehow pre-empts any further discussion on the subject, for the form is the very proof of the thought.

The neo-classical attitude to genius (and here Longinus is evoked) seems a little confused. Some, like Hobbes, seem to denigrate inspiration, others cannot help feeling that invention, imagination, gift, talent, genius and so on, are 'absolutely necessary' (Dryden) but they all agree on the need for observation, knowledge, apprenticeship, imitation of the best. To sum up: The poet is born and not made, 'Poeta nascitur, non fit', but, in the words of Pope:

> True ease in writing comes from art, not chance,
> As those move easiest who have learn'd to dance.

Typical of the underlying common sense of the age is Joseph Addison's balanced opinion on the free genius of a Homer or a Shakespeare and the controlled genius of a Virgil or a Milton. And equally typical is his fear of the double danger of wit (or *bel esprit*) and the stifling effect of imitation and rule. Augustan classicism, unlike French classicism which expressed itself completely in works of art, was very much a matter of critical utterance, and in the late Dryden, and in Pope, a matter of refinement, of attitude, of tone.

Another compromise is well illustrated by Rymer: 'Poetry is the child of fancy. . . . But fancy I think, in poetry, is like faith in religion; it makes far discoveries and soars above reason, but never clashes, or runs against it', and more racily by Dryden: 'nothing is more dangerous to a raw horseman, than a hot-mouthed jade without a curb'. The Earl of Roscommon *(An Essay on Translated Verse*, 1684) says the same thing in bad verse, and William Temple couches it in elegant prose. (One of the most balanced and lucid exponents of the Augustan age was undoubtedly Sir Joshua Reynolds, to whose *Discourses* (1786), the reader should turn. Irène Simon has not failed to pay tribute to, and quote from, this great painter and theorist.)

Reason, judgement, wit: the terms reappear suddenly, variously defined and permutated. Wit at its best is a novel, spirited way of expressing a truism, *Nature to Advantage Drest* (Pope), a path to truth. For Addison, who draws heavily from Boileau (and from D. Bouhours, *La Manière de bien penser dans les ouvrages de l'esprit*, 1687), good wit is that natural way of writing, the beautiful simplicity which we so much admire in the composition of the ancients (*The Spectator*, No. 62). Nature, truth and beauty are indissolubly linked: reason and experience prove it ... and the optimistic chain comes full circle. Feeling, already well marked, though differently, in La Bruyère and Pope, combined with the prose realism of the Enlightenment, was finally to break it and lead literature to other pastures.

Another aspect of the puzzle we are piecing together concerns taste. The debate as to the relativity of taste had gone on for a long time, when La Bruyère categorically stated that there was such a thing as *good taste*. The Augustans held the same conviction. Henry Home in his *Elements of Criticism* (1762) based his reasoning on a logical comparison: 'This conviction of a common nature or standard, and of its perfection, is the foundation of morality, and accounts clearly for that remarkable conception we have of a right and a wrong taste in morals. It accounts no less clearly for the conception we have of a right and a wrong taste in the fine arts.' Neither John Dennis, nor Addison, nor Steele, nor the third Earl of Shaftesbury, nor the philosopher David Hume would have found fault with this statement. Taste can be improved in the individual. For them, *de gustibus non est disputandum* would not have meant that taste was too subjective a matter for discussion to be worthwhile, but, on the contrary, that taste could be defined and even evaluated by an élite. We may have grown too sceptical to believe it ourselves, but we admit that the Augustan position was logical.

The rhymed couplet, put to good use by Waller and Denham,

praised and rendered more flexible by Dryden, found favour with Pope who brought it to its highest peak. It was deemed worthy of carrying the loftiest messages as well as the sweetest music conceivable at the time. Its dignity (Dryden's word) made it a fit tool for poets who knew their worth and claimed to be a force in the land, and its *closedness* (akin to that of the French alexandrine) was felt to be a challenge: how, they asked themselves, can we modify this – in itself – very restricted pattern? They gave their answer when they infused it with clear thought, cutting out redundancies found in looser forms, manipulating it until it could be made to say more or less anything, without killing the flow of imaginative thought: critical, philosophical, complimentary, elegiac or satirical. Reason had found a fitting way of expressing itself. Nevertheless, there lingered still the memory of blank verse, the heritage of Shakespeare and Milton. The defenders of blank verse, however, did not rely only on love of the past, they had a sneaking suspicion that to follow nature was not compatible with the strait-jacket of the closed couplet. Dryden, in 1664, expressed it thus: 'imagination in a poet, is a faculty so wild and lawless that, like an high-ranging spaniel, it must have clogs tied to it lest it outrun the judgement'. Four years later, Robert Howard questioned the validity of Dryden's statement: persons speaking *extempore* (in a play), are unlikely to express themselves *naturally* in rhymed couplets. Addison (*Spectator*, No. 39) is more explicit: 'I am therefore much offended when I see a play in rhyme'; 'common discourse' is often iambic but never rhymed. Traditional French prosody, is based on lines of eight, ten or twelve syllables, matched by the ten syllables of the English neo-classics: *even* numbers, which allow for the line to be broken into two symmetrical (and often antithetical) halves. *Blank* verse, on the other hand, is based on an *odd* number of stresses (five iambic feet) and it is interesting to note that French poetry reached its lyrical climax when Verlaine, in the 1860s, created for himself a flexible verse form based on odd numbers of syllables, thus breaking the stranglehold of the binary system.

All through the seventeenth century French society had whittled down the vocabulary it deemed fit for either polite conversation or serious literature. Modern readers are not a little surprised when they realize how few words were needed by Racine, La Roche-foucauld or Madame de la Fayette to clothe their finest poetry, intuitions and feelings. By the end of the century La Bruyère and Fénelon (*Lettre à l'Académie*, 1714), both realized that anaemia was setting in, and they both devised ways of energizing the language (by reviving old words, or by carefully inventing new ones). French survived, of course, but eighteenth-century poetry nevertheless suffered from the paucity of *acceptable* terms and from the clap-trap of worn-out mythological and pseudo-classical devices and imagery. The Augustans reduced their vocabulary too, but the parallel development of the novel, as well as the more liberal genre of satires, palliated the danger of crippling the language too much. Poetic diction went one way, towards an ever-increasing perfection, and prose another, keeping nearer to the ground and the live sources of the language. Johnson feared that even the most careful lexicographer could do nothing to prevent the decay of language, but with hind-sight we know that his fears were unfounded.

According to John Hughes (*Of Style*, 1698), words fit for poets must possess four qualities: 'propriety, perspicuity, elegance and cadence', and according to Johnson, speaking in the same vein some seventy years later, poetic diction was to steer a middle course, somewhere above good conversation and below the exoticism of strange words. As far as metaphors and similes were concerned, there seems to have been less agreement. John Sheffield (*An Essay upon Poetry*, 1682) warned against them; Dryden defended them (the 'figurative way is for the passions'); Addison, thinking in terms of the *sublime*, saw in metaphors a way of attaining it: from the Greek playwrights to Milton, all great writers have resorted to metaphorical speech, which was laudable, as long as no 'kind of an enigma or riddle' was produced.

All that has been said so far applies more or less to all kinds of writings favoured by the Augustans. Further to analyse the utterances of poets, critics, satirists and playwrights between 1660 and 1780 would take us too far. The student will find extracts of their various comments in Irène Simon's book, in which tragedy, tragi-comedy, comedy, opera, the epic poem, the pastoral, the ode, satire and translation are dealt with in turn. The actual priorities (of tragedy over the epic, for example) given by individual poets are of limited interest to the student of classicism as a whole.

The Augustan poetic world-picture is fairly consistent; it derives its strength from the equation of reason, nature and conscience. It is constantly, though not uniformly, propped up by reference to the great models of antiquity. What then was the accepted way of looking at the ancients? How could the challenge of the modern be met? How slavishly should one adhere to rules and precepts derived from the ancients? Were Christian subjects fit matter for tragedy? How could the proprieties of another time and latitude influence our sense of propriety? These and similar questions it was felt were waiting to be answered, and the answers were to be taken seriously.

The thinkers who did give answers were well aware of the difficulties; the ancients, so far removed in time and temper, were not easy of access, but the labour involved would be rewarded: the ancients had known nature intimately, and the passions, 'those springs of human nature', and the best way of moving 'pleasure in a reader'. In other words, the ancients taught a philosophy: that is, a psychology and a rhetoric; their rules are not arbitrary, lasting success is a proof of their excellence. In his

Essay on Criticism, Pope, talking of Virgil, sums up the lesson thus:

> Nature and Homer were, he found, the same;
> Convinc'd, amaz'd, he checks the bold design,
> And rules as strict his labour'd work confine,
> As if the Stagyrite o'erlook'd each line.
> Learn hence for ancient rules a just esteem,
> To copy *Nature* is to copy *them*.

This kind of utterance coming after Shakespeare and Milton does create in the reader an uneasiness which he does not feel quite so strongly when finding it in Boileau summing up the lesson of the French classics.

The real answer seems to lie in Young's paradox, according to which 'the less we copy the renowned ancients, we shall resemble them the more' (*Conjectures on Original Composition*, *1749*). What remains? A free imitation of a spirit, of 'high seriousness', tempered by a fine sense of humour. From a purely practical point of view, the young reader should be made aware that the study of the ancients is still rewarding *per se* and for a more complete understanding of modern classicism. (The 'Penguin Classics' may not be the best way of reading Greek and Latin authors, but they are *available* and *faithful*, more faithful than many seventeenth and eighteenth-century translations which, according to Pope, hover between literalness and paraphrase.)

I believe that a masterpiece arises from, and follows, its own law, a dynamic of its own, stemming from the temperament and aesthetic sense of its author. Modern man finds it rather difficult to imagine a whole generation building up a *body poetic* out of rules derived from works created in a by-gone age. Yet, the position of the Augustans was consonant with their philosophy. After all, they would say, the French had proved successful in their application of the rules elaborated by the Italians (thus perhaps missing the whole point of the originality of the French school). However ambiguous the average Englishman's attitude to the French imports ('foppery!') might be, French literature and mores did exert an influence. I would submit that French classicism was a temporary stumbling-block, a kind of temptation, put in the path of English writers. Dryden did not really succumb to it. Boileau, Rapin, Bouhours, La Mesnardière (*inter alia*) were discussed: they provided a sheet-anchor for experimentation, they contributed to the refinement of manners, language and poetry, as did rationalism, as did the sciences, as did toleration, as did also the new wealth of the merchant class ... not to mention renewed reading of Virgil and Horace. Pragmatic England could not give the same assent to rules as the French under the sway of their absolute monarch, nor would English writers so easily agree to co-operate with one another. The fierce literary battles of the French found only a reduced echo in the English world of letters: the famous quarrel of the Moderns and the Ancients, and so many others, all carried out over long periods of time. We follow them, as from a distance , in William Wotton's *Reflections upon Ancient and Modern Learning* (1694), in William Temple's *Essay upon the Ancient and Modern Learning* (1690): the discussions remained urbane, and possibly less detrimental to progress than the French battles of wits. The Enlightenment proved deleterious to tragedy, but it fostered new genres, because it was dynamic; it could boast of freedom and realism. Edward Young correctly claimed that the powers of the moderns were equal to those of the ancients, even if their performance fell behind those of Greece and Rome.

Sad to say, as there were rules – meant to be observed – the art of writing could be *learnt* in textbooks! Great artists would break them with impunity, but one cannot help wondering how many real talents were stifled by a pedantic and pedagogically attractive theory. (In this context one should look at the gentle figure of Fénelon, on the fence in the quarrel between the Ancients and the Moderns; see his *Letter to the Academy*, 1714, and, embodying

what sense of poetry he had in his prose-work, the delightful
Telemachus.)

Rules are deduced after the event; they produce nothing by
themselves. When Addison forced himself to write a classical
tragedy, *Cato*, he did not lack success, but already in 1713 John
Dennis showed 'the absurdities with which he abounds through a
too nice observing of ... (the rules), without any manner of
judgement or discretion'. Even Voltaire's best tragedies could not
alter the fate of tragedy in Europe.

One more remark is needed. Commenting on the marvellous as a
source of delight, Dennis said: 'Now the Christian machines are
quite out of Nature, and consequently cannot delight. The heathen
machines are enough out of Nature to be admirable, and enough in
Nature to delight. That which brings them nearer to Nature than
the Christian machines is the distinction of sexes, human passions,
and human inclinations.' Oddly enough, Corneille had burnt his
fingers when writing his Christian *Polyeucte*, and reverted to more
mundane subjects. In the classical scheme of things there was
little room for Christianity and its miracles. Transcendance and
decorum do not fit together somehow. You cannot legislate for
mysticism. (After *Tartuffe* Molière learnt not to meddle with
religion!) Decorum means prudence: here below, and off the
ground. Disproportion was scorned by Dryden; 'a king drolling
and quibbling' will not do, as Rymer puts it, and (to give Johnson
the last word): 'Sentiments are proper and improper as they consist more or less with the character and circumstances of the
person to whom they are attributed' (*The Rambler*, No. 140).

Classicism is evidently not a water-tight system; it allows for
much more variety and contradiction than an over-simplified
account might give it credit for. It does not muzzle dissenters.
Baroque, romantic and popular elements enrich it at least on the
periphery. Even Boileau, the most classic of the French classics, is
not without enthusiasm. When discussing the ode, he even went

so far as to claim for it a certain latitude: 'Chez elle, un beau désordre est un effet de l'art'. Assiduous reading of the French and English classicists allows us to penetrate the crust of formality and find a wealth of beauty, of flexible poetry, which modern prejudice hides from us.

8

Klassizismus und Klassik

Eighteenth-century German literature began with a swift reaction against the pessimism underlying the baroque of the second half of the seventeenth century, itself the aftermath of the Thirty Years War which had decimated the population. Rational and optimistic, based on the tenets of natural law and the works of Leibniz as propagated by Christian Wolff, it too emphasized the notions of common sense, normality, probability, nature, imitation and rule. Here again beauty, goodness and truth became equated, thus fostering the didactic purpose of literature. Not only did the whole movement look back to the ancient models, but it fed on French theory and practice, and also on English models such as *The Tatler* and *The Spectator*.

We find the same reaction against the baroque in Bach's extraordinarily controlled and structured music.

The mainstay of German Klassizismus was Gottsched (1700–1766), the upholder of good taste, the promoter of German as a literary language. Under him, 'art became a sector of philosophy' (A. Heussler, *Klassik und Klassizismus in der Deutschen Literatur*). Pedantic and despotic, Gottsched exerted a rather crippling though fairly short-lived influence on his contemporaries. We should not be too critical of him, however, as Germany was catching up with France and England and had to experiment quickly in all directions before it could find its feet and contribute to European literature. Gottsched lost touch with the deeper literary currents of his people, yet he had had predecessors, in particular Christian Martin Opitz, the translator of Seneca and Sophocles, who in his *Buechlein von der Deutschen Poeterei* (1624) had claimed the necessity of being well versed in Latin and Greek books, in order to learn the correct way of writing ('den rechten grieff'); who, as a pupil of Heinsius, had seen in antiquity the model of all art; and who had striven, already, to raise the status of the vernacular. The war put paid to possible developments along the lines of classicism, but Opitz's booklet never fell into disfavour.

The following quotation will illustrate Gottsched's basic attitude: 'The nature of man and the strength of his mind is the same as it was two thousand years ago: consequently, the way to poetic pleasure must be the same as that which the ancients chose so appropriately.'

And when he says *ancients*, we seem to hear also 'Corneille'. Rules and metre are regarded as leading towards harmony, peace and tranquillity. Without talent, without a real understanding of life and passion, they lead to the hollow drama exemplified by *Der sterbende Cato* (the dying Cato) and plays equally uninspiring. All was numbered, even tragedy!

Cartesianism, Leibniz's *Pre-established harmony*, Locke's and Hume's empiricism and sensualism, the deism of the age, and so on, all could satisfy the German thirst for ordered peace and method, but their equally deep need for expressing more homely emotions (*Gemütlichkeit* etc.) was soon to shake off the foreign shackles. Sorastro's victory over the Queen of the Night in *The Magic Flute*, was to prove short-lived. Gottsched had a methodical mind, his *Versuch einer kritischen Dichtkunst vor die Deutschen* (1730) provides an ample and well-formulated introduction to all the more stereotyped facets of neo-classicism, from close attention to detail to the stoical practice of virtue, imagination being given a wide berth.

Gottsched did not have it all his own way. J. J. Bodmer, in Zurich, agreed with much the German critic had to say, with his rationalism and didacticism for instance; but his freer mind found the Miltonian flight exhilarating; he saw no special virtue in alexandrines; nor was he prepared to prescribe for the poets. G. H.

Lessing (1729–1781) rose from the Gottsched school of writing to much greater heights, and succeeded in adding to the imitation of the French a keen interest in Shakespearian drama. It is to him that Germany owes the creation of a national theatre. If I bring Lessing into these pages it is not for plays (*Nathan der Weise* and the idea of tolerance, for instance) nor even for the rationalisations of the *Hamburgische Dramaturgie* where he goes over all the ground again, but rather for his *Laokoon* (1766) where, comparing painting and poetry, he discusses Winkelmann's dictum that what describes the essence of ancient Greek art is: 'Edle Einfalt und stille Grösse' (noble simplicity and tranquil stateliness; in *Geschichte der Kunst des Altertums*, 1764). This is significant in so far as the discussion centred for once not on literary matters, but on the plastic arts and in so far as the discussion illustrates the German preoccupation with Greece. In the period to be sketched out briefly, Greece played a much greater part than Rome, Corneille's Rome and his successors'. Most typical of this overwhelming feeling for Greece, is Hölderlin. The semi-romantic poet's love for all that the Mediterranean landscape stood for, sacred beauty, truth and goodness, perfect antiquity, is embodied in *Hyperion*, and many other poems, composed in what is possibly the most impressive German ever written.

Goethe's earliest work can be defined as rococo (one of the offshoots of artificial baroque); followed by the storm and stress period (Sturm und Drang, a kind of pre-romanticism which produced *Goetz von Berlichingen* and *Werther*, as well as Schiller's *Robbers*); itself followed by Goethe's *classic* period (if I may so simplify), in which *Iphigenie auf Tauris* was conceived (1779). This was finished in 1787, during Goethe's fruitful journey to Italy, where he experienced something akin to a re-birth ('eine Wiedergeburt'). Free to contemplate sun-bathed beauty, attentive to all the arts of the South, he acquired a sense of perfect equilibrium. The drama entitled *Torquato Tasso, Hermann und Dorothea* (the only successful epic poem in Europe since *Paradise Lost*), the *Roman Elegies* and so forth are the fruit of Goethe's subduing the more uncontrolled art and thoughts of his early manhood. The versified text of *Iphigenie*, epitomizes Goethe's original approach to tragedy. (For the use of verse in classical tragedy, see Steiner's discussion in *The Death of Tragedy*.) For sheer beauty, *Iphigenie* is nearly unsurpassed; the control of strong and vital emotions, the circumscribed setting (a holy shrine, between the King's palace and the island's coast), the loftiness of language and ideal, the gradual victory of enlightened humanity over barbarism: these are some of the features that make up this more meditative and lyrical, rather than dramatic, masterpiece of the period. The German term *Trauerspiel* (literally 'play of grief') fills the bill much better than *tragedy*: Goethe's deepest convictions lay in an educational idea, namely the development of the individual towards self-knowledge, towards knowledge of the great laws governing the universe, in practice, towards greater humanity, awareness and fulness of life. The process may be painful, but the final, often precarious moral victory (expressed as *Entsagung*, renunciation) of the great characters is far more convincing than the teaching, the explicit lesson, of his *classical* predecessors. Whatever struck us as too direct in previous tragedies has mellowed into that gentleness which one finds only in the *gentle* art of Racine.

Bildung and *Metamorphose* belong to a philosophy of becoming, to a conception of the world as changing for the better. Progress, albeit slow, does not fit strictly into the static picture of the world presented by earlier classicism. Goethe's more biological, Schiller's more historical and philosophical attitudes to life and art, their comprehensiveness, preclude the use of the water-tight categories accepted – as working hypotheses – by critics and literary historians. German classicism, a hundred years after Racine's *Phèdre*, rests on a tempering of Germany's harder self by the luminous humanity of Hellas.

F

9
Epilogue

Neither Racine, nor Pope, nor Goethe could have written surrealist poetry, or a novel of the American school, or Kafka's *Castle*: any of these genres would have appeared to them, quite literally, senseless. Our own predicament lies less in lack of comprehension of what the French and English classics were trying to do, than in a sense of frustration, even disappointment. Their works often strike us as cold, as lacking sensitivity. We must make an effort to overcome our reluctance. We have perhaps become too woolly, too romantic, or insensitive to their kind of sensitivity. We find it difficult to appreciate how much they themselves enjoyed their kind of poetry.

A writer adopts a form which is necessarily a compromise between what he feels, what he has to say (the subject-matter somehow chooses its own garb), and whatever forms are available. My experience tells me that I could not have formulated in prose the total message embodied in my poems. The classics discussed in this essay were originators of form within the limits imposed by tradition and the genius of their age. They would not have understood our difficulties when confronted with Boileau's or Pope's verse-epistles. Sophistication is such a shifting notion ...

At one point, I claimed that all literature bore the imprint of classicism. Less paradoxically, one could claim that all literature is either romanesque (it tells a story), baroque (it deals with deviation from a mean), romantic (by stressing the basic solitude of the individual) or realistic (photographic, and as such outside our scope). The permutation of these tendencies is responsible for the richness of European literature. Our particular theme appears to me to have been that of *crystallization*. For a hundred years, between 1660 and 1760, several generations of writers gave their well-nigh exclusive attention to summing up the human experience under a small number of rational categories. If Romanticism is ex-centric, then classicism at its literal best is con-centric.

> Thus God and Nature linked the general frame
> And bade self-love and social be the same.
> (Pope, *Essay on Man*)

Allegorically, the innermost circle represents a microcosm, image and likeness of the universe: a small medallion to the glory of Apollo.

Select Bibliography

This list of suggestions for further reading only contains fairly modern studies, which nearly all have substantial bibliographies, plus two or three very general books on literature.

General

ATKINS, J. W. H., *Literary Criticism in Antiquity*, 2 vols., Cambridge, 1934.

Critical Idiom Series

DIXON, P., *Rhetoric*, *1971*.

LEECH, CLIFFORD, *Tragedy*, 1970.

MERCHANT, W. MOELWYN, *Comedy*, 1972.

It is suggested that these companion volumes be read in conjunction with this volume.

HAZARD, P., *The European Mind, 1680–1715*. Translation available in Penguin Books, 1964.
European Thought in the Eighteenth Century. Translation, Penguin Books, 1965.
Brilliant analysis of an important transition period.

HONOUR, HUGH, *Neoclassicism*, Penguin Books, 1968.

KRAILSHEIMER, A. J. (ed.), *The Continental Renaissance, 1500–1600*, Penguin Books, 1971.
An excellent introduction to the century, which will serve as a basis for the study of classicism in the following centuries.

LOVEJOY, A. O., *The Great Chain of Being*, Harvard, 1936. Also available in Harper & Row *Torchbook* series (paperback).
A full study of a theme dear to classicists; an important link in the history of ideas.

Penguin's Companion to Literature series

DAICHES, D. (ed.), *British and Commonwealth Literature*, 1971.

DUDLEY, D. R., and LANG, D. M., *Classical, Byzantine, Oriental and African Literature,* 1969.
One of the best series of reference books on the market.

THORLBY, A. K. (ed.), *European Literature*, 1969.

STEINER, GEORGE, *The Death of Tragedy*, London, 1961.
Perhaps the most personal and enlightening study of the genre.

French Literature

ADAM, ANTOINE, *Grandeur and Illusion: French Literature and Society 1600–1715*, trans. H. Tint, London, 1972.
See Part 2, Section 7. Stresses the creativity of the French Classics.

BENAC, H., *Le Classicisme*, Paris, 1949.
Similar to Irène Simon's book in intent, but less ambitious and rather over-systematized.

BENICHOU, P., *Morales du grand siècle*, Paris, 1948.
Indispensable for a good understanding of the century.

BORGERHOFF, E. B. O., *The Freedom of French Classicism*, Princeton, 1950.
A very original approach to non-classical features of the seventeenth century.

BRAY, R., *La Formation de la doctrine classique en France*, Paris, 1951.
A ponderous work, very scholarly and a little confusing.

BRODY, J. (Ed.), *French Classicism: A Critical Miscellany*, Englewood Cliffs, N. J., 1966.

CRUICKSHANK, J. (Ed.), *French Literature and its Background*, Vols. 2 and 3, Oxford, 1968 and 1969.

FIDAO-JUSTINIANI, *Qu'est-ce qu'un classique?* Paris, 1930. Charming, wordy and not very useful for a beginner.

MOORE, W. G., *The Classical Drama in France*, Oxford, 1971.

PEYRE, H., *Le Classicisme français*, New York, 1942. Studies the elements which *together* make up French classicism, and is partly applicable also to England and Germany.

SAINTE-BEUVE, *Port-Royal*, 3 vols., Gallimard (Bibliotheque de la Pléiade). The masterpiece of biographical criticism, the most exhilarating account of the grand-siècle.

WRIGHT, C. H. C., *French Classicism*, Harvard, 1920. Clear and to the point, but a little old fashioned.

English Literature

ABRAMS, M. H., *The Mirror and the Lamp*, Oxford, 1953.

ATKINS, J. W. H., *English Literary Criticism:*
The Medieval Phase, London, 1952.
The Renascence, London, (2nd edit.) 1950.
Seventeenth and Eighteenth Centuries, London, 1951.
The classic textbooks on the subject after Saintsbury, Spingarn, Ker, Smith, etc.

CLIFFORD, J. L. (Ed.), *Eighteenth Century English Literature*, Oxford, 1959.

GORDON, G. S. (Ed.), *English Literature and the Classics*, Oxford, 1912.
Elegant studies of Greek and Latin influences on English literature at different periods.

GRIERSON, H. J. C., 'Classical and Romantic' in *The Background of English Literature*, London, 1934.
A re-examination of the two movements.

HAMILTON, K. G., *The Two Harmonies*, Oxford, 1963.
Study of the nature and function of prose and poetry in the seventeenth and eighteenth centuries.

JONES, E. D. (Ed.), *English Critical Essays: XVI–XVIII Centuries*, Oxford, 1922.

SIMON, IRÈNE, *Neo-Classical Criticism*, London, 1971.
Provides the easiest approach to the Augustan critics. Systematic without being in any way pedantic.

TRICKETT, R., *The Honest Muse*, Oxford, 1963.
A very convincing study of Augustan poetry.

WARREN, AUSTIN, *Alexander Pope as Critic and Humanist*, Gloucester, Mass., 1929 (reprint, 1963).

WATSON, GEORGE, *The Literary Critics*, London, 1962.
A description of the patchwork quilt of literary criticism from Dryden to Leavis.

WELLEK, R., *Concepts of Criticism*. New Haven, Conn., 1963.
Like Wellek's other works, an indispensable tool for the study of critical terms and the history of ideas.

WILLEY, BASIL, *The Seventeenth Century Background*, London 1934.
The Eighteenth Century Background, London, 1940.
The English Moralists, London, 1964.

German Literature

CLAUSS, W., *Deutsche Literatur*, Zurich, 1944.
A simple outline, little bibliographical material.

FRIEDERICK, W. P., *An Outline History of German Literature*, New York, 1948.
A brief outline and a very fulsome bibliography.

HEUSSLER, A., *Klassik und Klassizismus in der deutschen Literatur*, Bern, 1952.

MASON, G. R., *From Gottsched to Hebbel*, London, 1961.

STAHL, E. L., and YUILL, W. E., *German Literature of the Eighteenth and Nineteenth Centuries*, London, 1970.
See in particular the bibliography.

STRICH, FRITZ, *Deutsch Klassik und Romantik*, Bern, 1962.
A very beautiful and penetrating book.

Index